Paddling South:
Winnipeg to New Orleans by Canoe

RICK RANSON

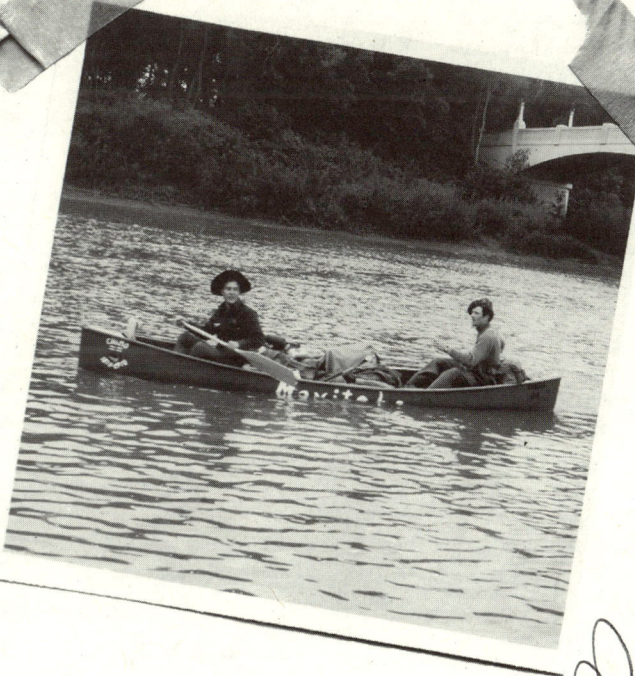

NeWest Press

COPYRIGHT © RICK RANSON 2007

Library and Archives Canada Cataloguing in Publication

Ranson, Rick, 1949–
Paddling south : Winnipeg to New Orleans by canoe / Rick Ranson.

ISBN 978-1-897126-23-3

Ranson, Rick, 1949- --Travel--Red River (Minn. and N.D.-Man.). 2. Ranson, Rick, 1949- --Travel--Mississippi River. 3. Landeghem, John van--Travel--Red River (Minn. and N.D.-Man.). 4. Landeghem, John van--Travel--Mississippi River. 5. Canoes and canoeing--Red River (Minn. and N.D.-Man.). 6. Canoes and canoeing--Mississippi River. 7. Red River (Minn. and N.D.-Man.)--Description and travel. 8. Mississippi River--Description and travel. I. Title.

FC3395.R3R35 2007

917.127'4043

C2007-902694-X

Editor for the Board: Ross Jopling
Text Editor: Carol Berger
Cover and interior design: Natalie Olsen
Author photo: Image 2 in Winnipeg

Alberta Foundation for the Arts

Canadian Heritage   Patrimoine canadien

Canada Council for the Arts   Conseil des Arts du Canada

edmonton arts council

NeWest Press acknowledges the support of the Canada Council for the Arts and the Alberta Foundation for the Arts, and the Edmonton Arts Council for our publishing program. We also acknowledge the financial support of the Government of Canada through the Book Publishing Industry Development Program (BPIDP) for our publishing activities.

No bison were harmed in the making of this book.

NeWest Press
#201 8540.109 Street
Edmonton, Alberta
T6G 1E6
(780) 432-9427
newestpress.com

1 2 3 4 5 10 09 08 07

printed and bound in Canada

▼

THIS BOOK IS DEDICATED TO

Isabel

Mary Lou

Joanne

who taught me how to treat a lady...
or else.

▼

▼

Lake Winnipeg

MANITOBA

Lake Manitoba

Winnipeg

Letellier

Lake of Woods

Pembina

...na River

Red River

Grand Forks

Mississippi River

Lake Winnibig...

...smarck **Fargo**

MINNESOTA

Bois de Sioux

Brainerd

Lake Traverse

Big Stone Lake

Minnesota River

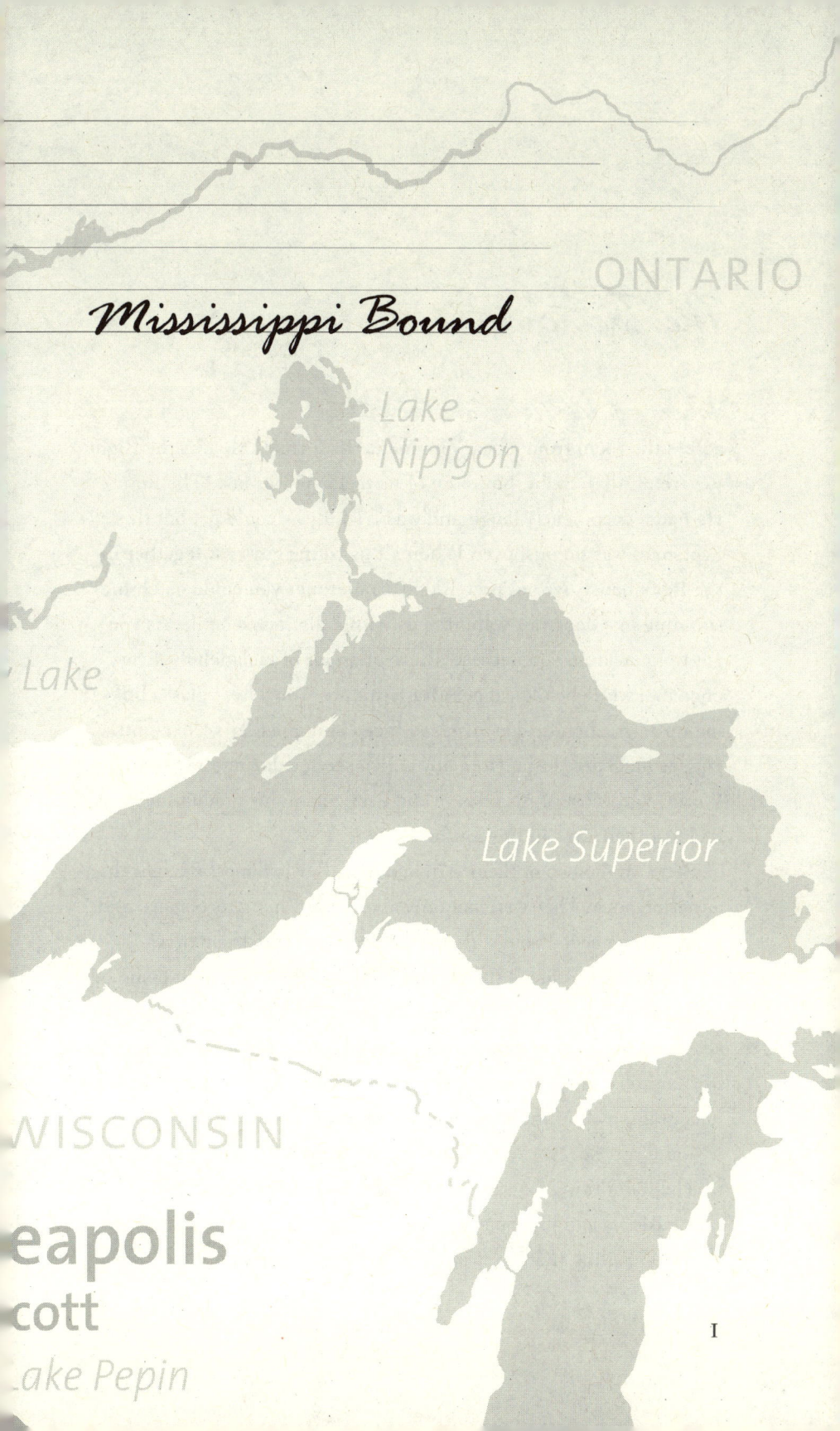

Mississippi Bound

ONTARIO

Lake
Nipigon

Lake

Lake Superior

WISCONSIN

eapolis

cott

ake Pepin

The Tactician

John and I sat cradling sweet tea
across the room from a bear of a man. His formal title was the Right
Reverend Allan Selby, but to all of us teens he was just 'The Rev'.
He had a deep hearty laugh and was friendly as could be, but this
Scotsman was no pushover. When all us young guys got together in
the Rev's house, we got pretty loud. Sometimes you could catch him
standing in a doorway, watching us with a distracted smile. As you
got to know him, you became aware of an air of melancholy. Every
once in a while he'd disappear for a minute. You'd hear glass clink-
ing upstairs, then he'd return, red-faced and quiet. His Coke-bottle
glasses had barred him from any active service during the Second
World War. Most of his friends and everyone in his graduating class
had lost their lives in the conflict.

Between the two of them, Mr. and Mrs. Rev had more degrees than
a thermometer. They were not only book-smart, but street-smart, and
so when we needed help with a problem, we went to them first.

Our problem started the second week of July, when John made his
first contact with the Centennial Corporation. The Corporation was
set up by the government to oversee the hundred-year anniversary
of Manitoba joining Canada. It was spending barrels of tax money
encouraging all Manitobans to start up centennial projects, which
it would sponsor. We took them at their word.

The main thing we wanted from the Corporation was help in
purchasing a suitable boat we could use to paddle our way to New
Orleans. Failing that, we wanted it to help us promote the trip in

some way. If we couldn't get that, our fall-back position was to get a letter of introduction addressed to the various governments along the route.

After two months of pounding on highly varnished doors, all we got were promises. We came to the conclusion that the government didn't want to know us. They didn't help us promote the trip. And no letter was ever going to come. The Corporation wanted us to go away. Fortunately for us, it failed to recognize the subtle, sly, and downright dirty tactics a church minister could employ. What we got from The Rev was far more valuable than any handout from the civil service — what we got was a lesson in government guerrilla warfare.

"Rev, we talked with this guy five, six times."

His eyes sparkled through a cloud of pipe smoke.

"It didn't happen."

"Yeah, it did. Five times at least."

"It didn't happen. I've had bank managers lie to me. Heck, I've had other ministers lie to me. I'm an expert in lying," he chuckled. "If you don't write it down, it didn't happen. After you meet with someone, you always write them a letter. The secret is to record names and dates. Who promised what, and when they said they'd do it."

"Well, okay."

"Not just okay. A letter is proof. Just make sure," he pointed with his pipe, "you are the one writing the letter."

"Okay."

"And don't be stupid. Keep the original, send him a copy."

"But Rev, this guy was really enthusiastic. He thought this trip was great. He promised us money for a boat. He promised to promote the trip, write letters ..."

The Rev was quiet for a moment as he puffed on his pipe.

"And do you know why he was enthusiastic?"

"Why?"

"Because he wasn't the one who made the decision. He didn't

give a tinker's dam, pardon my french. He just wanted a friendly way to get rid of you."

"John, I think we've been screwed."

"You know, Rev, we could never nail this guy down …"

"A Talleyrand?"

"A what?"

"A who. Talleyrand. Charles-Maurice de Talleyrand. He was the ultimate survivor. He was in five French governments. He was a minister for Louis XVI and Marie Antoinette until they got their heads chopped off, then Napoleon, Louis Phillip, the Bourbons … Napoleon was supposed to have said, 'You are shit sir, shit in a silk stocking.'"

"Rev, watch your language."

He smiled.

"Now this is what you do. Go to your city councillors for letters of introduction. After the meeting, send them all notes, thanking them for their efforts, and mention you'll be at their offices Friday to pick up the letters."

"What about the Centennial Corporation?"

"We'll get to it, laddie, we'll get to it soon. With those letters in hand you go down to your local MLA's office, and talk to the nice lady who runs the place. Show her the letter, tell her your problems."

"Not the MLA?"

"No, you don't need to. The woman runs the place."

Mrs. Rev looked up from her desk and smiled.

"You see, lads, all governments hate each other. You want them to compete for your project. If the province sees that letter from the city, they'll go off like a flare."

Obviously enjoying himself, the Rev stopped to refill his pipe.

"Next, you write a note explaining your project, and you take it to the papers. You talk to a reporter and you tell him that the Centennial Corporation has been extremely slow, nothing more. You want them to move, you don't want them mad."

"But Rev, that guy gave us nothing but the runaround."

He held up his hand.

"It didn't happen."

"Okay, okay."

"All newspapers hate each other too. So you make sure *The Press* knows that *The Tribune* is your next stop."

John and I glanced at each other. We were sitting at the feet of a master.

"Now, give it a day, maybe two, and go back to the Corporation. By this time our friend has had phone calls from two city councillors, one MLA, and two newspapers."

"We'll have his undivided attention."

"No you won't. You'll be talking to his boss."

"I love it when you talk dirty, Rev."

Both the Rev and Mrs. Rev straightened.

"It's a joke."

"Oh."

Some people can make "oh" mean a lot of things.

"A couple of things — when you talk to the newspapers, be spot-on accurate. These people have antennae. They'll crucify you if they think you are lying."

"We won't lie."

"Everybody does, laddie. Sooner or later."

"We won't."

"Second, and the last piece of advice for tonight," he said, glancing at Mrs. Rev and slowly nodding, "finish what you set out to do. Because if you pack this trip in halfway, everybody who supported you will feel betrayed. They'll never let you forget that you chucked it all."

"We won't quit."

"You'll want to, lad, you'll want to."

The Start

WINNIPEG FREE PRESS,
TUESDAY, SEPTEMBER 16, 1969

Cruising Down the River

It's a long way to New Orleans. Rick Ranson, 20, and John Van Landeghem, 20, both of St. James-Assiniboia, are preparing to make the trip this fall — in a 16-foot fiberglass canoe. They estimate they should arrive in New Orleans about Christmas after three months of paddling. The boys plan to depart from the Assiniboine Park Foot bridge Saturday and proceed down the Assiniboine to the Red River, from there to the Minnesota River, and on down the Mississippi. The trip, which is more than 1,500 miles by car, has been made by canoe at least twice before, once in 1900 and again in 1967. They will carry letters of introduction from Mayor A. W. Hanks of St. James-Assiniboia, the Manitoba Centennial Corporation and Premier Ed Schreyer, as well as 200 pounds of luggage and food.

Saturday September 20, 1969

"Got everything?"

"I think so. Even if we've forgotten anything, we'll be within driving distance for a couple of days, Mom."

It was a kaleidoscope of emotions. I picked up my two knapsacks and looked around my bedroom. All the planning, the dreaming, the talk, all the staring at my worn Rand McNally road map in the middle of the night, had crystallized into this day.

For me, travelling was second nature. By the time I was fifteen I had lived in ten different houses. Dad was an officer in the Canadian Air Force and it seemed like every two years we packed up and moved. Every two years my brothers and sisters became my only friends. Every two years I had to fit into the hierarchy of a new group of kids and start a new school. As a result, my mobile family became extremely tight and remained so. I learned to make quick but super-ficial friendships, and I still hold the record for some of the worst marks ever achieved in various schools across Canada.

One thing I did learn, and learned very well, was how to wander. I once bedded down in a church basement in Vancouver with a cadre of fresh-faced communists bent on my conversion to the faith — the destruction of capitalism and the setting of new copulation records. I politely turned down the advances of a homosexual on Detroit's Woodward Avenue and enthusiastically attended one of the first love-ins in Griffith Park in Los Angeles. I meandered through the streets of Tijuana, Mexico, and was included in a wedding party in Butte, Montana. All this before I was eighteen.

One of the high school books we were forced to read was *Huckle-berry Finn*. It may be corny, but Mark Twain's description of life along the river caught my imagination like no book had. The Mississippi River flowed through *Huckleberry Finn* like a thread, tying all the stories together. It seemed easy — stay with the protection of the river and when you want to meet people and have adventure, just pull up to the riverbank. With one small portage, the Assiniboine River that flowed by my parent's house would be a starting place to eventually join the Mississippi.

We unloaded the knapsacks and camping gear from my father's 1965 Ford station wagon by the footbridge that crossed the Assiniboine.

"Gee, look at all the people."

"I count fifty, maybe fifty-five."

"Fifty-six." I still had a teenager's eagerness to correct my father.

"Hey Rance, there's the guy from the Centennial Corp ..."

Remembering what Napoleon had said to Talleyrand, I yelled out, "Hey Ed. How ya doing? Nice stockings. Silk, right?"

John and I smirked at his puzzled expression.

It was a day between the seasons that captured the best of both. Not a cloud in the sky, soft breeze, and warmth on our back. No bugs, no mosquitoes — it was perfect. The green from the trees was a dark, late-summer hue. Here and there a leaf flashed orange. We ignored the early fall warning.

We loaded up the canoe and with a kiss to our mothers and a cheery wave to the crowd we began to leave. Just then a photographer came out from the local paper to take our picture as we sculled backwards, getting into position. With a cheer from the crowd we set off.

"She didn't come to see you off."

"Nice of you to point that out. Maybe she had to work," I lied. John was just pointing out the obvious, but it still got to me.

We hadn't accomplished a thing but we felt fulfilled, like we had finished a grand adventure, and not just begun one. It was like finally getting that date with the prettiest girl in school. She was clean and fresh and new, just like we had imagined. John and I paddled past the rich neighbourhoods, taking a perverse pleasure in looking into people's backyards, their dirty laundry land. One of the richest houses on the richest street in Winnipeg dumped their lawn garbage unseen to the world at the river's edge, waiting for the spring flood to wash it away. Here and there footpaths, hidden from the busy streets, made their way down to the shore. The glint of tossed bottles shone in the sunlight. Two dark and silent vagrants slowly nodded as we paddled by. I wondered if the owners of the fine houses we passed knew that drunks were using their backyards for trysts.

We paddled to the confluence of the Assiniboine and Red Rivers. At the fork was a jungle of trees cut by footpaths that led to and from the old CNR warehouses — a magnet for carousing derelicts.

The north-flowing Red River tugged at the canoe, slowing it down, making us pay for every stroke. A breeze sprang up, slowing us more. The late summer sun danced off the flickering waves. All day we paddled. By the evening we passed the Winnipeg City Limits sign.

"We're going slower than I thought."

"Who cares? We're paddling south."

Winnipeg to the Border

The transistor radio,
perched on top of the tarp that covered our backpacks, was dying
a slow death due to the cold and wet (and constant use). But every
once in a while, the signal would strengthen and a song would
come on that echoed our idyllic situation. An overwhelming sense
of adventure surrounded us. The fall colours along the banks of
the Red were brilliant, the sun on our shoulders warm, and a
gentle breeze heavy with the smell of rich clay wafted over us.
It was great to be alive.

That lasted about two days. On the evening of the second day
out of Winnipeg, it started to rain. It wasn't a deluge — it was just a
torturous-slow-cold-steady tapping on the tarp. Not enough rain to
make you decide to stop and set up camp, but enough to slowly soak
you through. The bread in the bottom of the knapsack turned to a
blob of white glue.

Creeping along, we passed little Manitoba town after little
Manitoba town — St. Adolphe, St. Agathe, Aubigny, Morris, St. Jean
Baptiste, Letellier. Our heads bowed to the drizzle as we pushed the
river behind us, the little towns too high up on the riverbanks and
too busy with their own concerns to notice a passing canoe. We
ignored each other.

The banks of the Red were mud the consistency of half-chewed
bubble gum. They were high and steep — an advantage when we
wanted to get away from the wind and the rain, but a prison when
we wanted to actually get out of the boat. We often paddled for an

▼

hour or more before finding a suitable place to camp that wasn't
a clay fortress or a barrier of burrs.

"Hey Rance. You know I figured it out and we're averaging 13.8
miles a day."

"Nice."

"Well that's not bad considering all the gear and shit we have
to haul around."

"What's the date today?"

"September 24th."

"We're going to have to average fifty, sixty miles a day to get out
of this cold, John. We ain't gonna make it at thirteen miles a day."

"Well anyway, tomorrow we'll hit the border."

It rained all night. John's hands were blistered and infected and he
sniffled and coughed all the next day. His nose was red and tender, his
hands were red and tender, and his feelings were red and tender.

"I think we're here, John."

"Where?"

"I think we hit the border."

"Why are you so sure?"

"Look."

"What?"

"Look at the beer cans. They're American. Park the boat and we'll
find the Pembina border crossing."

"Radio's dead."

"Figures."

You're a Duck, John

The only sounds

were the soft *plunk* of paddles dipping into the water, accompanied by
the occasional *slurp* of the river being pushed behind us. Yesterday's
winds had petered out overnight, leaving a strange, uneasy silence.
Scraggly oaks, with bowed heads still and silent, deep green-blue in
the fall sunlight, stood resigned to the coming winter. Every now and
then a dry leaf high up in a tree would twist back and forth, its rus-
tling accentuating the hush.

First one, then two, then a line of clouds, like a herd of elephants,
glided in from the northwest. Shadows disappeared and the day turned
to gloom. These clouds came on slowly, ponderous and deep. They
would stick around a while; they were low and dark with moisture.

You can tell when rain clouds change to snow. There's a bite to
the wind. Before the first snowfall people cup their ears, seeking
temporary warmth. They sniff and hack and spit, and pull out the
old cedar-smelling winter parka — the one that they spilt beer on at
the last high school football game. There's frost on people's breath
that's whisked away in the breeze. Perfectly normal people stop,
grunt, and, staring off into the clouds, make pronouncements about
the weather that a Sioux medicine man would admire. The smell of
autumn leaves fades as nostrils contract with the cold. Snow clouds
are whiter at their edges than rain clouds.

When it snows in the Dakotas, it stays. Not like Kansas or Oklahoma
— blizzard one day, melt the next. The first snow of the year usually
comes around Halloween. It wouldn't snow today, but it was close.

It was a day at the end of one season, sliding into another. A tired day, a changeable day, a day made for contemplation. Our canoe floated down the river just outside Grand Forks, its occupants lost in thought, mesmerized by the constant stroke of the paddles.

"You know, John, I been thinking."

"Oh good."

"I've been thinking about you and me and why we are on this trip — our place in the big picture. And you know what?"

"What."

"I think you're a duck."

"Huh?"

"You're a duck, John."

"That's what I thought you said."

"And you know why you're a duck?"

"No, but I'm sure your going to tell me."

"Because you always look so calm on the outside, but deep down everything's churning. You're kicking like hell. I've never met a guy with more going on under the surface, who shows it less. You're a duck, John."

"Just paddle."

"Don't you think?"

"If you say so."

"I know so."

The Red is a tired river, slow and lazy. Sometimes deep in South Dakota it even seems to stop, trickling over a beaver dam like the twitching of a dozing cat's tail. Even when it floods it does so slowly. It periodically drowns farms and ruins lives and every once in a while it even kills the odd daredevil, but for the most part it just drifts. The clay gumbo it cuts through is as flat as piss on a plate so the river can pretty much meander anywhere it wants. It glides back and forth, probing for something to bump into.

"You're crazy."

"Sorry?"

"You heard me. I said you're crazy."

"I'm crazy?"

"Yeah."

"Is that because I said you were a duck?"

"Well ... yeah."

"John, we've been paddling for a friggin hour and that's what you been thinking of?"

"Well ... yeah."

"Okay, I'll bite. Why am I crazy?"

"Well, most normal kids get summer jobs. You? You hitchhike to Mexico. You flunked grade eleven — twice — but you read all the time. You're always doing something, but it's never the thing you're supposed to be doing. You're crazy."

"You mean I'm a cauldron of contradictions?"

"Well ... yeah."

"It's all been said before. Stand in line."

"You prick! I've been thinking about you for an hour and you talk to me like I don't matter!"

"I didn't mean ..."

"Screw you, Rance!"

"Sorry."

"Fuck you."

Nobody spoke. An hour later we paddled past a farm. An American flag hung limp on its pole. It seemed odd to see the flag in front of someone's home. When you see the Stars and Stripes in Canada, it's in front of a business, and it's hung there as an invitation, not for any patriotic reason.

The high riverbanks had given way to a gentle grassy slope. A small wind puffed at our faces, a relief from the stillness of before. The farm's cattle stood in the sun, watching us glide past, chomping cuds in a cow chorus line.

"You're all gonna die!"

"They're milk cows, Rance."

"Nice tits, ladies!"

"That's what I mean! You're always joking but you're never happy. Not really. You hide behind jokes."

"Fuck you, John, just fuck right off."

"You know I'm right."

"I don't want to talk about it."

"You're crazy, Rance."

"You're a duck, John."

The Fargo City Jail

The door had weight and momentum.
I imagined fingers guillotined as it swung shut with a *clung* that
made the floor and walls vibrate. It didn't open very often.

The bars were never warm. They were thick to hold but decep-
tively easy to grasp. Grabbing them, the first instinct was to pull
my face as far out of the cell as possible. If I could get my nose
outside of the bars, I could at least *smell* free. They pressed cold
lines down the sides of my head, framing my view. Letting go, a
sticky residue covered my hands and face. Grease from a previous
inmate — wonderful.

The toilet stuck out of the wall like a stainless steel bagel. There
was no seat. They hadn't removed it, it came that way. The toilet
faced the hall. I couldn't cover myself with some clothing or even
hide behind my bare legs. I crouched naked, pants at my ankles,
legs spread, facing the guards and the other inmates. Anyone could
watch my most private function, and they did.

The taco-thin mattress smelled like a cross between ammonia
and a civil war bandage. The bed frame was cleaned periodically,
but the mattress was soiled constantly. At first, the bleach from the
sheets was all I could smell. After a while, the bedding warmed up
and other smells oozed. When I woke up, the smell of all the other
inmates who ever slept on that thin slab of canvas was plastered
to my skin.

Ceramic tiles covered the walls and the ceiling. They made it
easier to hose the cell down. At first, the tiles were all I noticed.

▼

A closer look revealed the writing between them — tiny messages calling out from the pale grout. From the floor to as high as a man could reach, names, dates, salutations, and curses were scratched into that grout. Standing on the free side of the bars was too far away to see the graffiti. Lying on the bunk, the pain from all the cell's previous occupants was inches away: Dale G ... 14 months, Randy H ... 8 months, Lionel B ... is a rat, and the all-encompassing Fuck U!

The guard passed by the cell.

"I gotta lock you guys in for the night. That's the rules. If you need anything, just call."

"When is lights out?"

"Lights out is when you close your eyes."

Fargo, North Dakota. The Civic Office Building was right down by the Red River. John and I wanted to see where we could camp close by, so we walked in the back door. It turned out that the Fargo Police Department was in the basement of the Civic Office Building.

We decided to ask the desk sergeant for directions before trying to deliver the letter of introduction to the mayor. He gave us the once-over as we got closer to the head of the line. I'd seen warmer eyes in a bait box. We'd been crawling through Red River mud for five days and looked it. John wore his knife at his belt. When it got to our turn, we started to blurt to the sergeant who we were and what we were doing. Quietly, three very large blue uniforms assumed positions on either side of and behind us.

"We're paddling up the river and we're ..."

"Which one?"

"Which one?"

"Which river?"

"Oh, that one. The Red."

"Where'd you come from?"

"From Winnipeg and we're ..."

"You paddled up the Red River from Winnipeg?"

"Yeah, and we're look—"

"Hey! I saw you on TV!" One of the cops almost shouted. Everybody jumped.

"Where's your canoe?"

"Out back and we're ..."

"On the river bank?"

"Yeah and we're looking ..."

"Hey, let's go look!"

"... for a place to sleep."

Two minutes later, half a dozen policemen, a couple of grubby Canadians, and several curious onlookers were gathered at the riverbank looking at the canoe. Traffic slowed on the highway that ran past the building as drivers craned their necks. We were peppered with questions. These guys were pros at asking questions.

"How long did it take you?"

"Three weeks from Winnipeg."

"Where'd you sleep?"

"In a tent, out on the riverbank."

"Where'd you eat?"

"Brought the food with us. John's a pretty good cook and I like to make coffee. We shop in the towns we pass."

"Where do you stay when you get to a town?"

"Well, that's why we came to you. Usually we grab a hotel close to the river and clean up. But we're running low on cash, so we're looking for a park, or this riverbank. There's a laundromat over there."

"You can't stay on this property."

After a moment, the sergeant spoke up.

"Hell, stay with us. We got room."

The rest of the policemen joined in.

"Sure, sure, we got room."

"Where?"

"In a cell. C'mon."

The sergeant had a slight frown.

"Today's Monday — you gotta be out by Thursday."

"Why?"

"We get busy on Thursday. We got our regulars."

It was decided. The policemen picked up the knapsacks and the canoe and walked into the jail. John and I looked at each other. Before we could even accept the Fargo City Police Department's offer, our gear and canoe had been incarcerated.

The cell door slammed. A sucking feeling, like being pulled beneath black water, wrapped its icy bands around my chest. I breathed in gasps. Biting off chunks of air and swallowing claustrophobia, I heard the guard's footsteps down the hall and watched his shadow disappear into the radio sounds of the squad room. Then we were alone in our individual cells with our bottled panic.

If we called, would the guard come back? Was this imprisonment real? Was it some kind of cruel trap?

"Johnny?"

"Yeah?"

"Quite the resort, eh?"

"I think I'm gonna be good forever and ever amen."

"Yeah, I'm gonna stay as clean as an angel's panties."

"John?"

"Yeah?"

"These cops are pretty decent."

"Well, they're letting us stay here free."

"Yeah, but you know what surprises me most about these guys? They're office workers. I figured there'd be more yelling. More attitude. Like on TV."

"You mean being a cop is a job? Go figure."

"Screw you, Johnny."

"John? You get the feeling that these cops could make your life a living hell and still stay within the rules?"

"How so?"

"Well, I mean if someone was giving you a hard time, you could wash the floor in front of his cell with pure ammonia. Then he'd have to bury his face into this piss-smelling pillow for an hour or two."

"Or you could give him his supper, watch him eat it, then laugh."

"How about not giving him toilet paper?"

"Naw, just soak it in water. Then give it to him."

"How about playing Mozart on the radio when the guy likes Johnny Cash?"

"Or slamming the door to the next cell in the middle of the night?"

We slowly drifted off to sleep.

Screams. Screams and moans and babble and shouts. I shot awake in my bunk as several men were led into the drunk tank. They were feet away. I heard them, smelt them — I could almost feel them. But I couldn't see them. One screamed. I heard the gut growl and the splash of someone throwing up.

"Don't hide behind that friggin badge! Come on in here and face me! C'mon! C'mon!"

It was a sound riot for an hour. I tried to cover my ears with the piss-smelling pillow in a vain attempt to get back to sleep. The screaming and the crying came in fits and starts. Eventually, it lessened by degrees. All except for one guy.

"Oh Gawd, forgive me."

"Shaddap!"

"Oh Gawd, forgive me."

Many voices.

"Shut the fuck up! Shut up! Shut up! Shut up!"

"Oh Gawd, forgive me."

"Shut up an' go ta sleep!"

"Oh Gawd, forgive me."

"Shadddappp!"

"Oh Gawd ..."

Whap! Thud!

"Ouch. Aaeee!"

The sound of doors opening and heavy boots running down the

hall gave me a start. Several shouts and screams later, the cops gave the fighting drunks a final warning. When they left there was a long pause. Sleep even seemed possible.

"Oh Gawd, forgive them."

Even the cops laughed.

Overland to the Mississippi

"You're quiet, Rance."

"What do you expect, I just got outta jail. Those guys in the drunk tank just wouldn't shut up. I haven't slept in three days."

"I had no problem sleeping."

"That's the difference between you and me, John. You'd make a great convict. You can sleep anywhere. Besides ..."

"Besides what?"

"I'm not too pleased we're getting to the Mississippi by car."

"Station wagon."

"Car."

"Rance, for Pete's sake we ran outta river!"

"Yeah, I know, but it's a compromise. Sometimes it's pretty hard to sleep in the bed you've made."

"Where did you hear that?"

"What?"

"The part about sleeping in your own bed."

"The desk sergeant."

"I knew you didn't make that up yourself. You do that lots."

"What?"

"If someone says something offbeat, you repeat it."

"Quit being so picky. Besides, no matter who said what, we're still getting to the Mississippi the easy way."

"Don't be stupid, there was no more water."

"It was a compromise, John."

"A small one."

"Yeah, you start with one small beer at Stewart's house and you end up screwing the girls's volleyball team."

"You screwed the girls's volleyball team?"

"NO! What I'm saying is you start off with one small compromise and then another, and another, then that's all you're doing. You end up calling it a compromise, but really it's cheating. It's cheating, John."

"It was nice of the cops to get us a ride to Brainerd."

"They needed the cells. It was Thursday night."

"It was nice anyway."

"It was the girls's swim team."

"What?"

"It was the girls's swim team."

"You made it with the girls's swim team? Really?"

"Jeez John, you'd believe anything. What colour are the clouds in your world?"

"You do have a way with words, Rance."

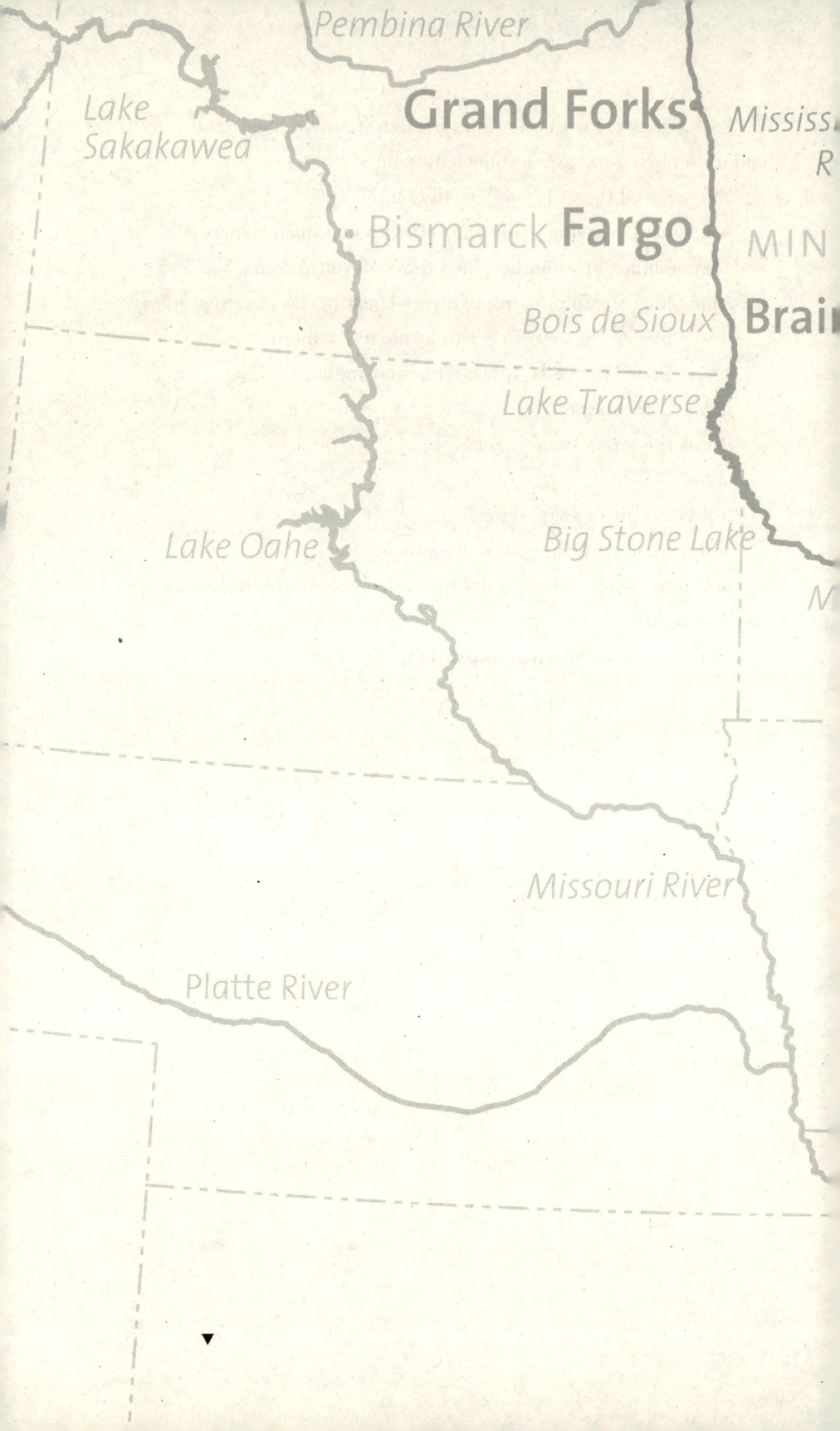

Pembina River

Lake
Sakakawea

Grand Forks

Mississ.
R

Bismarck **Fargo**

MIN

Bois de Sioux

Brai

Lake Traverse

Lake Oahe

Big Stone Lake

N

Missouri River

Platte River

Upper Mississippi

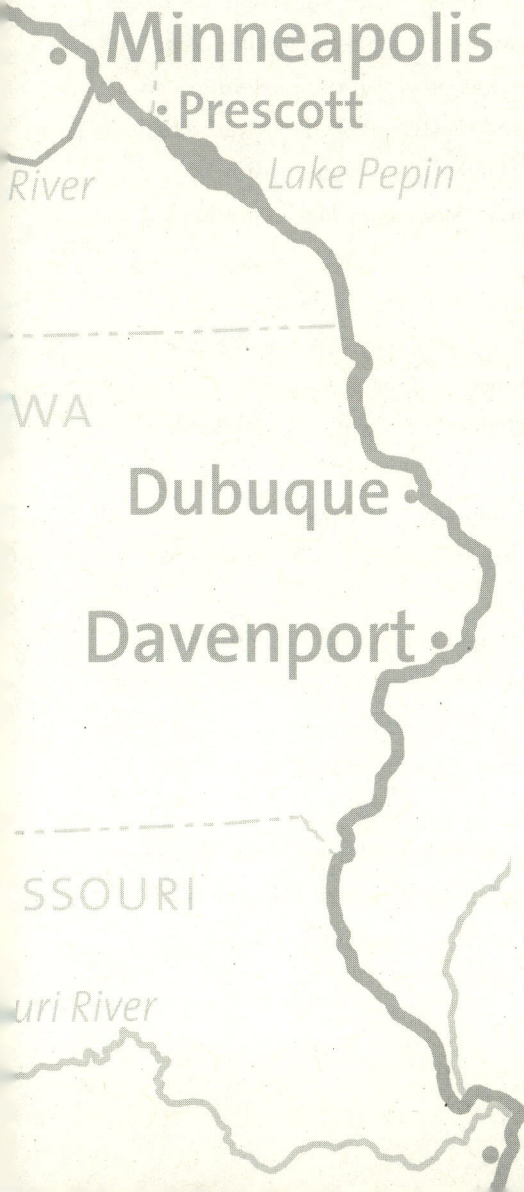

Minneapolis

• Prescott

River

Lake Pepin

WA

Dubuque •

Davenport •

SSOURI

uri River

An American Boy

To me, it wasn't Ol' Man River at all.

From where we put in at Brainerd all the way to Minneapolis, I thought of the Mississippi as a young man — strong, muscular, confident.

The Upper Mississippi River was powerful in a mischievous way. The water was clean and fast and boisterous. It dived and rolled as it played between the hills. Sometimes it would throw us high in the air as it tumbled over rocks, and sometimes it would slow to a calm.

For the first time on our trip, we could really hear the river. It would slurp over the rocks, fizz and crackle when it trapped bubbles, and thunder over rapids and dams.

Up close, the northern Mississippi is the colour of iced tea, steeped from the roots of a million pine trees. Through the amber the rocks and sandy riverbed gleamed up at us. Our chests tightened as we saw how close the white granite outcroppings came to our fibreglass bottom.

And the smell. It was pungent and heavy, and clung to us in the morning like a spiced humidity. Sometimes it was scented with pine from the trees along the banks and sometimes it was sweet from the grasses. Once in a while a nearby farm contributed its particular odour, but always there was that earthy smell.

We rode the young river, passing neat little towns with no-nonsense names like Little Falls, Sauk Rapids, Elk River, and Coon Rapids. Pioneers christened the features they encountered as they ventured deep into the northlands wilderness.

Just north of Minneapolis we paddled by a powerhouse. The river suddenly turned warm. It was discharge from the powerhouse and was really just purified water, but the heat felt unnatural. There, the Mississippi was vacuumed into a fifteen-storey boiler, screened, filtered, de-mineralized, scalded into steam, turned into super-heated steam, squeezed to an unbelievable pressure, hammered through turbine blades, cooled, and returned to a liquid. It was only water, but it was inert, distilled — all living things removed.

After a mile or so the tepid water returned to its natural, cooler temperature, but the young man didn't seem quite so playful anymore.

Can You See Anything?

"Can you see anything?"

"How the hell can I see anything? I'm sitting at the back!"

"What's that?"

"Some truck starting up. Must be a mile off."

"We must be in the middle somewhere."

"What's that?"

"Tree branch stuck in the water."

"Looks like a snake. We must be moving pretty good for it to make that slurping noise."

"More like a ripping sound. Current must be doin' five miles an hour."

"At least."

"We're paddling about five, so we must be doing about ten."

"As fast as a man can run."

"Where the hell did this fog come from?"

"Water's warmer than the air."

"Ah shit, that's all we need."

"Snow, friggin, snot-sucking, pain-in-the-ass snow."

"Shit."

"Shit."

There was a girl in high school who had prominent eyes. It looked like she was constantly startled. Her nickname was Road Kill because she looked like a deer caught in a car's headlights. Road Kill had this huge ball of backcombed hair and several layers of mascara that highlighted the whites of her eyes. It was like she was daring you to notice them. I glanced back at John. He had Road Kill's eyes. He looked back at me. I had them too.

"I'd say let's head for shore if I knew where it was."

"With all the crap and trees falling in the water, we're safer out here."

"Where's here?"

"Minnesota."

"Yeah, I know that, but where?"

"Upper Mississippi."

"You're just a Niagara Falls of information, John."

"You know, if we tip, we don't even know which way to swim."

"Have you felt the water? We'd freeze to death before we got to shore."

"I've been in white-outs before, but I'll remember this one. We could get sucked into a powerhouse, or over some rapids, or a falls ..."

"John."

"What?"

"Shut up. You're scaring the crew."

"John?"

"What?"

"Your eyes are better than mine. Are you sure you can't see anything?"

"All I can see is white. White snow, white fog, white rain — all white. Water's black though."

I'd get into a rhythm. The canoe rode like a '53 Cadillac, all soft and heavy. The paddles were silent, except for the odd gulping sound. My arms and back were warm with movement and pulsing blood. The canoe rose up and forward in a slow sensual cadence, settling between strokes but still gliding forward. There was a slight hiss as the two-inch bow wave sliced the river. The water was just above freezing but the palms of my hands wrapped around the paddle were warm. In the chill river air, steam from our efforts rose off us, dissipating bit by bit, whispering away. Silence and the paddle's beat slowly put my mind in a state of serene emptiness. Hours passed and I was lulled by the swish and sway. Stroke, stroke, stroke.

"Watch out!"

"Left! Left!"

"C'mon!"

"We must be close to the bank."

"No shit! I just about got beheaded by that dock. Let's find another one and wait this out."

"My sleeping bag is soaked. I can't stop for the night. I need to find a town with a laundromat. Let's keep going."

"Okay, but just remember — I'm the one that'll be sucked into that powerhouse intake first."

"Yeah, yeah. You want some cheese with that whine, Rance?"

"John?"

"What?"

"I never liked you."

"John?"

"No, I don't see anything!"

"John?"

"What!"

"Do you hear that?"

"No. Well I heard voices a while back. High up. Must be a cliff around here."

"I hear something — kinda like a helicopter before you really hear it. I feel it."

"It's a motor."

"Big motor."

"Traffic."

"Train."

"Yeah, it's a train."

The current increased. Something stuck deep in the river broke the surface. We stopped paddling and watched it shoot by. It disappeared in the mist and snow. I held my paddle flat, outrigger style, in an attempt to regain control. There was no movement from John so I knew he was doing the same. Water boils welled up and jostled the canoe, sending it zigzagging all over the river.

"I can't see a thing."

"Sure can feel the river though."

Our paddling slowed, becoming tentative. The river had changed. I would stroke and there would be no resistance. Once, I pulled the paddle out of the water and looked at it because I was sure something had grabbed it. Blindfolded, we rode the dragon.

"That's a long friggin train."

"Real long."

"You think it'd be gone by now."

"It's gotta be close, even the air's shaking."

"Finally. Look, it's the bridge."

Out of the fog and snow of the late afternoon gloom the black shapes of pylons rose from the mist. The river smoothed out. Strangely, the fog was thicker on the other side of the bridge. Beyond the pylons was only white. Even the black river disappeared.

"It's a dam! It's a dam! That's not a bridge! Back! Go back! It's a spillway!"

"Jeeezzzus Murphy!"

"Hurry! Turn around! Go back!"

"Come on ... come on ... come on! Harder! Harder!"

"Over there! Angle over there! Pull!"

"Harder! Harder!"

We hung on for several minutes as the current pulled us towards the rumbling invisible. We paddled. Oh God, how we paddled. We just couldn't beat the current. It was faster than we could paddle. From deep down we pulled. The thunder from the water roared in our ears. We dug and pulled and clawed. Achingly slow, we moved at an angle from the brink. Like a python releasing its prey, the reluctant river spat us out at the side of the spillway.

We followed the lip of the dam and ran the boat up the riverbank to a grassy picnic area. For long minutes we hunched in our canoe, still but for our heaving chests. I stared at the snowflakes melting one by one on my shaking hands.

Minneapolis

Almost a month after leaving Winnipeg, we arrived in Minneapolis. Sometimes, when we were up to our knees in the mud of North Dakota and in the snows of the Upper Mississippi, it seemed we weren't paddling so much as digging our way south. This voyage had to get better.

We paddled up to the Northern States Power Company powerhouse in downtown Minneapolis, blown in by a windstorm with our damaged canoe slowly filling with water. I saw a log float over the St. Anthony Falls. It was captured in the grip of the water swirling at the base of the falls. Sometimes it would almost break free but it would always get sucked back to resume its slow, watery waltz.

All the gear was soaked and needed to be laid out for a couple of days to dry. The canoe needed to be repaired in a warm, dry place for the patch to cure. The NSP people kindly let us do that. Throughout our voyage, we encountered many people who would try to help us or offer advice. In Minneapolis, it seemed everyone was that way.

We were going to stay at the YMCA and dry out. We needed time away from the canoe, but most of all we needed to sleep away from each other. We had two days to pick up the mail and any money sent from our parents. We wanted to visit the Corps of Engineers to see if someone there would brief us on what to expect of the river, and we needed to buy detailed maps of the Mississippi. Up until then we had been using the good old Rand McNally and following the little blue squiggle. We needed to shop for groceries, dry the clothes and the gear, and in any spare time write thank-you letters to all the people who had helped us along the way.

We met a businessman friend-of-a-friend who invited us to supper at an expensive restaurant. When John and I arrived we were the only people in the red velvet-walled room who were not wearing dark banker suits. The maitre d' smiled in our direction, betraying the fact that our host must have warned him of the impending appearance of two scruffy derelicts. John and I smiled at each other, our faded blue jean jackets flickered in the reflection of the crystal and silver.

"Beats the lunches in the tent, eh?"

"What, you don't like my cooking?"

"No John, your cooking's great, I just think this steak is missing something. Ah yes, it doesn't reek of propane."

Our host smiled. He was at least fifty — he was old. His suit was dark, plain and worn. The elbows and the seat of his pants were shiny.

He was interested in our trip, our lives, and our country. But I noticed that he shifted in his seat. He shoved the food around on his plate. Either he was uncomfortable with us, or something was bothering him. We didn't have to wait long to find out.

"I have a friend. Nice family, churchgoers. His son got his draft notice, and yesterday, without saying anything to anybody, just up and left. Went to England. His mother's quite upset about it, but his father, my friend … it's … it's as if the kid died."

Our host looked at us, his two hands working the fork's handle, the last word hung in the air like a sigh.

"I know there's draft dodgers in Canada," I said, "but you don't see them too often."

"Yeah," John chimed in. "They all go to British Columbia or Toronto."

"They keep a pretty low profile. Like it's not something you advertise."

"The family's just … devastated."

"If he went into the military how long would he have to serve?"

"Couple, three years."

"This is the type of thing that people remember." I looked at John. "You know Grand Beach and Pine Falls?"

"Sure," John said.

"Well, during World War One, a great uncle of mine took to the woods and spent four or five years trapping with the Indians up there."

"So?"

"Well, he died a couple of years ago. And almost to the day he died that was thrown in his face. People remember that kinda shit."

There was an audible exhale from our host. He stared at the disturbed but uneaten dinner.

"That's a forever decision."

We continued to eat in silence for a time, but after a while John and I steered the conversation to our voyage, into safer waters. The old man brightened and asked why we were waiting around — was it to take a rest?

"No, we're waiting for mail from home that should contain some money."

He reached into his pocket and handed us enough money to last a week. He laughed when I asked him whether this donation was to help us out, or just to help us out of town.

After dinner, he drove us back to our rooms at the YMCA. I glanced out the window of his luxurious car. St. Anthony Falls still had that log in its black grip.

The next morning friends of John's parents invited us into their home and let us wash our clothes. While we waited, they let us phone our families in Canada as the mother fixed us lunch. They were a typical family — a father, a mother, a pre-teen daughter and a son in high school. They weren't rich like the businessman, but just the same, Vietnam entered their conversation easily and constantly. Vietnam was like living downwind from a hog farm. No matter what you did, every day you'd get a whiff. Sometimes the wind would change and fresh air would tease you, but sooner or later the smell of pig shit would come back. When the topic of the war came up, or when the mother looked at her son, who was less than a year away from military age, she crossed her arms in front of her and toyed with some imaginary pearls at her throat.

At the end of the day, while sitting in a restaurant over coffee talking about our errands, a young couple came and stood unannounced at our table. The boy was skinny and forgettable, but the girl had a healthy glow that would stop conversation when she entered a room. Her eyes had that frantic shine of the newly converted.

"You guys coming to the Moratorium?" she asked us.

"Moratorium?"

"Yeah, the march against the war in Nam. We're marching against the *establishment*," she spat the word out. "You musta seen the posters." Her eyes widened in disbelief.

"No, we've been camping for the last month. And our radio died."

"Well there's gonna be thousands of people, all marching against the war. Here's a poster. It's gonna be a blast."

"That's encouraging."

She gave us a sharp look like we'd taken somebody's name in vain.

John and I watched her body jiggle as she inched away. Suddenly she jumped and waved at some other young girls entering the restaurant. Our eyes followed her as she walked over to the newcomers. They chirped away like chickadees. The boy stood by us, watching them. Before he left he leaned over and gave us a conspiratorial nod.

"You gotta come, there ain't nothing hornier than a girl at a demonstration. Last demonstration I got balled three times."

All three of us turned and looked at the fresh-faced vision across the restaurant. Then the boy walked over and put his arm around her waist, his hand on her hip.

John and I sat staring into the dregs of our coffee.

"You know what we would be demonstrating against, eh?"

"The war."

"Partly, but mostly it would be against all those people who have been giving us money, taking us to lunch, and inviting us into their homes. That's the establishment."

"You know, John, this thing is tearing these people apart. All we see on TV is the bombs going off. You don't see the businessman trying not to cry or a mother wrapping her arms around herself with worry."

"The only guy who thinks this is a joke is that fucker over there running around with his cock in his hand."

John and I looked at the young couple. The girl saw our look and came back, her attitude harder than before, her fresh face taut.

"You coming?"

"I'm sorry, we can't."

Her mouth opened up, but before she could fling an insult, I spoke.

"We're Canadian. And if the cops ever picked us up at a demonstration, the least of our problems would be we would never be allowed back in the States."

"Oh." She seemed to shrink. Then she slid into the seat beside me. I was aware of her leaning against me.

"What does Canada think of the war?"

John and I looked around, wishing the question would go away. After a long pause, I said, "I can't speak for all of Canada but most of the kids in my school think that, well … it's your war."

"Yeah, we're your friends, we'll hold your coat, but this is a problem the US is going to have to solve."

"That's why we gotta be there." She waved the poster. "We gotta."

When we left the powerhouse early the next morning we paddled upstream to give St. Anthony Falls a wide berth. The log was still tumbling and rolling, trapped in the grip of the cascading water. I had visions of paddling upstream into the falls just to dig that log out with my paddle. I realized that it would free itself in its own time, and in its own way.

Just out of Minneapolis the river is straight, fast, and clean. High white cliffs gleaming in the afternoon sun dominate the east shore.

This is what we had come for. The sky was cobalt blue, the air crisp. Leaves on the trees rattled on the bank from the wind at our backs. Paddling was a joy. It was just us and the river.

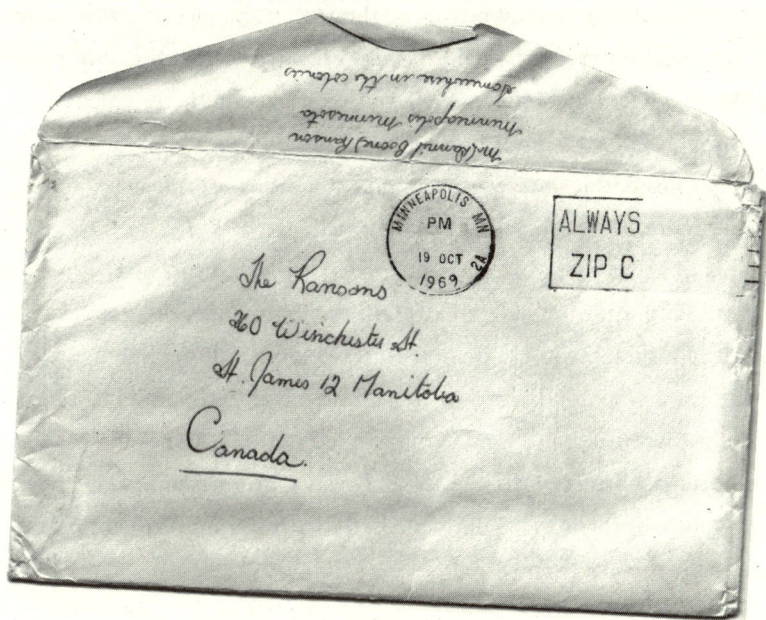

Lake Pepin

Lake Pepin is a place

where the Mississippi River slows enough and widens enough to
be called a lake. On the map it looks like a fat banana. There are
hills on the Minnesota side that rise gently from the shore and
disappear into the horizon. The Wisconsin side of the lake has two
features: Long Point and Point No Point. Point No Point says it all.
Approaching from either direction, you get the distinct impression
you are approaching a point of land. The closer you get, the more
you realize it's a sandy beach that just keeps on going — an optical
illusion of sorts.

We paddled down the middle of the river channel and, with some
foreboding, entered Lake Pepin. We were surprised at the abruptness
of the change. One moment we were loafing along the middle of a
channel, the next we were far out in the middle of a lake. Our paddling relaxed, the water was millpond smooth. This was going to
be a breeze.

It's not that we didn't have a choice — we just didn't make the
right one. John wanted to go straight down the lake, the quickest
route. I thought it might be best to stay close to shore. Seeing no
need for a course change, we continued out into the middle. The
wind, what little there was, barely flicked our hair. As we got further
into the lake, the wind slowly rose. It was a bright, sunny day and
the gentle puffs behind gently pushed us further and further into
that wide brown expanse.

A wave folded over on itself, rescuing my mind from autopilot.

Awakened from my daydreams, I noticed little wavelets gently plopping all around us. My stomach tightened. If there were waves here, how big would they be at the far end of the lake?

I looked behind us and stared at the waves. John instantly picked up on my thoughts. He silently looked around. We searched the Wisconsin side and the Minnesota side — both were much too far away. We made for Wisconsin.

The wind started to whistle in my hair. I felt the back end of the canoe rise as John fought a wave, trying to control the boat. I rose up as the wave passed underneath. The canoe shuddered down the backside of that brown roller. We no longer searched longingly for the shore — we went into survival mode. The harder we paddled, the longer we could remain safe in the troughs of the waves. Water slopped over the sides of the canoe as each wave passed. We surfed the front of the wave and paddled like hell in the trough.

On the peak of another wave we washed into a sandy beach, finally making the safety of Point No Point. I jumped out and splashed through the water, dragging John and the canoe in a frantic effort up onto the sand. John jumped out and together we heaved the boat and gear well above the high-water mark of the waves.

I could hardly walk because of the cold and fear. We made a crackling fire to warm up and help keep the dread away. We crowded near the flames and slowly thawed out. Lunch was made and coffee was drunk. We stood looking out across the lake to Minnesota. I looked at John, his back to the fire, his wet clothes steaming.

"I've been thinking, John ..."

"You want to quit?"

"No. No, I was thinking about Mark Twain."

John stared at me like I had lost a chunk of my mind.

"Huh?"

"Mark Twain was a steamboat pilot. He looked down on this river from three decks up. He was thirty feet away from the water."

"So?"

"He was inside a nice warm pilot house. No wonder he loved this river. He didn't have to sit in it!"

John watched me, his eyebrows knitted.

"We've been fucked by Huckleberry Finn!"

John shook his head and turned to the fire.

The wind dropped and on the white sand it was almost hot. The fire was abandoned. We sat on the beach through most of the morning and watched the rollers slowly disperse.

"I got circulation back." John signalled that he was ready to continue.

We huddled on Point No Point, halfway down the lake on the inside curve. We had to pick our moment and make for the end of the lake as fast as we could. If the winds started up again, it would be much worse this time, because the wind and waves had a good ten mile shot at us.

We repacked the canoe and tied the cover tight. We pushed off from the sandy beach and turned our canoe south. We estimated the far shore, the Minnesota side, was about four miles. With a slight wind at our back it would be an easy paddle. We were fifteen minutes into the lake when I glanced back at John. He looked terrified. Over his shoulder, gusting over the hills on the Minnesota side, was the blackest, meanest looking thundercloud we had seen for weeks. It covered the sky like a huge, angry jellyfish, its tentacles dragging across the landscape. I did some quick calculations. The squall was ten miles away, bearing down on us at about twenty miles an hour. We were over three miles away from the shore, doing five miles an hour. We would still be on the water when it hit us. We were screwed.

With the monster rumbling down on us we paddled as hard as muscles and blood could propel us. The waves got bigger and bigger the further out and more exposed to the wind we became. This time we didn't worry about the water splashing in. The fact that the sky became black told us that the thunderhead was winning. We had been in the canoe for over a month so we were experienced in all kinds of water conditions, but nothing like this. We were a cork in a washing machine. Gone were the steady, evenly spaced rollers. The waves bouncing back from the far shore smashed into the waves being pushed from the thunderhead, and we were stuck in the middle.

A wave splashed into the canoe. We slowed, beginning to wallow. The only way to safety was to put our backs into paddling and dig the lake behind us. Wind whipped John's voice. I could only make out one word—"Rain!"

I snatched a glance and was instantly sorry. Less than two hundred yards behind us was a grey waterfall crashing from the clouds. The rain hit with such force that I was pushed over, slapping the paddle on the back of a wave. The pouring rain slowed the canoe by the minute. I didn't want to stop and try to bail. Maybe if I denied its existence, the rapidly rising water would go away. I pulled on the paddle so hard I expected it to snap in half.

A rock flew by under the canoe. There was another one, then another. I looked up and we were headed right into a rocky beach. There was no finesse, no watching for sunken logs, we bullied our way over the rocks. When the canoe scraped bottom I jumped into that October water and grabbed the bow. Right beside me, pulling the canoe far up onto the rocks, was John. Fear, relief, and release caused us to shout, yell, laugh, and slap each other. Then we just stood there, watching the rain come down on Lake Pepin.

The Night Boat

It was cold in the morning,
but compared to North Dakota it was a heat wave. We woke up to
forty-eight Fahrenheit, with the temperature rising to a high of fifty-
four in the afternoon. We passed through some pretty countryside
around Prescott and Diamond Head, on our way to Dubuque. It was
a perfect day for paddling — a fast tailwind, a deep, narrow channel,
cool, clear blue skies, and plenty of scenery.

We camped in a natural park far away from civilization. The oak
trees formed a wedge bordering an open sand amphitheatre. The
canoe was pulled up into the orchestra pit. The main stage, with its
constantly moving and changing moods, was the Mississippi. The
temperature was below freezing and the condensation from our
breath hung suspended in the tranquil air long after we had exhaled.

We sat on the beautiful sandy beach between the tent and the fire.
It was as still as a church on Wednesday. The full moon, the crackling fire, and the stars so close you could steal them. We spoke in
hushed voices.

"What's that?"

"What's what?"

"That noise. It shimmers. It's not a truck — too big."

"It's not a dam. We'd know a dam if we heard one."

"Damn right."

"It's a barge."

It was a river barge, working its way against the current toward us.
Sometimes you could hear it distinctly. Sometimes, when it turned in

the river, the motor was muffled and quiet, but the growl never went away. It kept growing. The engine, deep inside its iron ribs, rumbled. We turned our heads in an attempt to capture the sound.

The noise kept coming. We sat by the fire like two little boys waiting by railway tracks while an invisible train rumbled towards them. What is it that makes people enjoy the anticipation more than the realization? Does your mind paint pictures clearer, with deeper hues, than reality? We wanted the barge to come faster, but knew that the waiting was the best part.

On it came. The glow of its lights flickered and painted the other side of the valley. Trees that had disappeared in the sunset reappeared in flashes. Finally, it swung around our bend. The sound, once muffled and wavering, was harsh and sharp. Its lights flashed as it pushed the river before it. Red, green, and orange lights near the bow and a constantly moving searchlight made it appear otherworldly.

The searchlight hunted us down, striking with a physical jolt, almost painful in its intensity. The brilliant cold light scanned our campsite. We were examined like specimens under a microscope — classified, noted, dismissed.

The sound changed from a deep growl to a harsh metallic whining. Our bodies resonated to the sound of the giant motors. As it slowly rumbled by, the sound changed to a deep-throated thud of twin exhausts. Its lights, once sharp, slowly dimmed and then faded to black.

We stood and watched the sound go. Its rumble decreased to a murmur, then nothing. In its wake a sound shadow lingered, blocking out any other night sounds.

We were suddenly very cold.

An American Working Man

Starting at Minneapolis,
the river turns into a working man. It's no-nonsense — confident and
sure of its power. With its sleeves rolled up, it's aware of its position
in the scheme of things. It's grown up, this American working man,
and it's wearing work boots.

Grumbling towboats with their barges plod in a procession up and
down the river, carrying corn, iron ore, oil, and gasoline. They pass
docks, cement factories, and grain terminals. The weathered steel
buildings track the edge of the river like castle towers.

Just south of Minneapolis and stretching all the way to St. Louis,
the Mississippi's flow is blocked by over two dozen lock and dam
structures. Every twenty odd miles the river has a barrier across
it with a large lock built in. The original purpose of all this was to
allow unfettered barge traffic to Minneapolis. The designers and
builders of those structures had but one aim — move cargo to market,
pure and simple. Due to the slowed current, large lakes had formed,
adding to the valley's beauty. Every once in a while, somewhere along
this stretch, you could find an inlet, a spit of land, or an island that
was untouched, empty. Sitting around a campfire, watching the stars,
one imagined that the last footsteps that had graced that sandy beach
wore moccasins.

The exuberant current north of Minneapolis, rocketing back and
forth between the river banks, was replaced by a steady, resolute march.
No more high spirits, but a whole lot more river. The Mississippi didn't
burble over hidden rocks here. It was immense, powerful, and silent.

One of the advantages of being in a canoe was getting a feeling for the country we paddled through. From a speeding boat, a dark spot in a grey riverbank could easily be missed. From a canoe that grey spot was something to be explored. We'd discover it was the mouth of a small creek with a tiny, sandy beach hidden by trees. We'd scull under the overhanging branches, interlaced like a church ceiling, and enter a half-lit world that only raccoons, deer, and heaven knew about. As the shadows of great steel barges passed unaware, we'd set up camp in a cove as pristine and untouched as ever there was.

With the afternoon sun warm on our faces, we paddled by places with names like Lake City, La Crosse, and Davenport. The sparkling reflection of the sun on the water was complemented by the silver leaves on the trees, clattering on the cool north wind. Rolling hills made the river bend just enough to make us wonder what was beyond.

Incident at Lock 20

It was a night when people who worked outside wished they didn't. Clouds were low and unseen. Raw wet wind came over the trees along the Mississippi like a wave, stealing warmth from the bargemen. Noses were red and runny. Hunched men made great noises hacking and spitting. They held their ears and wiped their noses with giant leather mitts.

John was sick. He lay in one of the towboat's bunks gasping and wheezing. I guessed he was getting rundown.

I was working with Jerry, the mate on the towboat *George W. Banta*. He had the kind of teeth that made you wish he wouldn't smile. In the hours that Jerry and I worked together he regaled me with stories of running guns, piloting jets, and strafing Cuba. Then there were the stories about how he'd been in jail three Christmases in a row, been a member of the KKK, and had numerous women (all of them naturally infatuated with him). He'd beach bummed in Mexico, and had been a master sergeant in the United States Air Force. He was now out of jail on two years' parole for having dynamited a building.

"Why'd you blow up a building, Jerry?"

"An affair of the heart, my northern brethren, an affair of the heart."

Then he threw his head back and laughed so that his confederate general's goatee pointed at me like a dagger.

Marie, the cook, leaned over and whispered. "You gotta understand Jerry. Sometimes he lies through his tooth."

"Oh really," I whispered back.

I followed Jerry across the barges, handing him rope when he wanted, pulling cable when he wanted, and listening to his stories, which he wanted most of all. We worked steadily until we came upon Lock and Dam 20, just north of Canton, Missouri. It was but one of twenty-seven locks on the Upper Mississippi.

The tow consisted of sixteen separate barges loaded with sixteen thousand tons of grain. It was 1,200 feet long and as wide as a football field. To wrangle a one hundred and five-foot-wide tow into a lock one hundred and ten feet across was no small accomplishment. What was so amazing was the delicate manner the bargemen employed to manoeuvre that leviathan.

To fit through the lock was a two-step process. The entire tow was double the size of the lock so the sixteen barges had to be broken into two sets of eight and sent through separately. The tow was placed exactly right in the lock and then secured. The back half that stuck out was removed. The gates closed on the front half and it was lowered through the lock. It was then pulled out with giant winches and anchored, waiting to be reconnected with the back half.

As we stood at the front of the tow, with the pilothouse a quarter of a mile back, Jerry spoke into the microphone.

"You have twenty feet to the end of the lock, captain. You have fifteen feet captain. Now you're coming into ten feet, captain. Nine … eight … five … two and a little bit, captain … about six inches now … OKAY!"

Twelve hundred feet of steel and the barge captain and his mate parked it within six inches of where they wanted it. As soon as the captain commanded, all that was heard was the clanging of steel on steel as the bargemen disconnected the spider web of cables so that the tow could be split. When they finished, the engine of a towboat thundered in the distance and the back half slowly pulled away.

Jerry and I stood on the rust and dirt of the deck of the back half, watching the secured barges in the lock recede. Another day was dying and the raw wet wind spoke of an early winter. I stood with my back to the wind watching the Mississippi as we eased upstream. For a moment it seemed that Jerry was going to say something profound. Squinting towards the towboat, he tensed.

"Oh, oh."

"What do you mean 'oh, oh'? I don't like it when someone who knows more than me says 'oh, oh.'"

"Look out there."

In the glitter of the searchlights on the water, the towboat and the tow started to swing sideways. The captain was trying in vain to swing the six hundred feet of barge into the current. Even in the confined space of the lock's approaches, waves jumped the rusted side of the barge. An intense look crossed every crew member's face. The towboat's engine screamed deep inside the vessel. Nervous glances were cast — even a casual worker knew this could get hairy.

"If we get caught in the spillway current this is going to get real dangerous real fast."

Jerry started to back away from the rail. Not really understanding, but respecting my companion's experience, I followed. He watched the approaching dam like it was something deadly. The once straight line of barges bent in the current like a banana. Cables started to crack and groan like a falling tree.

"Get down!"

I hunched over.

"No, NO! Like me! On your stomach! Those cables are going to give!"

I gingerly lay down on the cold and icy deck, staring at the cables. They seemed okay to me. The tow continued to bend and the cables began to *crack-crack-craaaaack* ... *BANG!* Where a steel cable the thickness of a man's wrist once was, there was nothing. It slashed back, hitting the barge where we had stood just seconds before. It left a frisbee-sized dent in the quarter-inch steel plate. The whole barge rang like a muffled bell.

"Another one's going, get as low as you can!"

"I can't get any lower, my zipper's in the way!"

Crack-crack-crack ... BANG!

"JEEEZZZTHATTWASCLOSE!!!"

"I hope you get paid well for this!"

"It's a living."

Pieces of cable, flecks of white and red paint, and a cloud of rust settled to the deck where we lay. The barges groaned and muttered to themselves as the current dragged them towards the dam. A city block-sized barge thumped the cement spillway. Of course, this was hard to see with my hands over my head and my cheek resting on a steel barge deck.

"Break's over! I'm running back to the pilothouse. You coming? You might as well — all the cables have broken already."

"You bargemen sure know how to show a guy a good time."

They gathered at the edge and looked over the rim of the dam at the thundering water in the spillway. It sucked the barge to the dam like a giant vacuum, holding it solid. Finally, the captain dragged the vessel along the side of the dam past the spillway's suction to where he could regain control. The second, ultimately successful attempt to dock at Lock 20 was a lot slower than the first.

It took us hours to stitch the broken barge with new cables and another hour to pass through the lock. Once we were safely through, we had to rejoin the two halves of the tow. Most of the night was spent pulling cables, tightening winches, pulling, pushing, straining.

I didn't know what time it was when I finally got back to the compartment, but the sky in the east was light. John woke up when I came into the room.

"You shoulda seen what I saw," he croaked. "I was lying in my bunk looking out the porthole and I saw this dam coming closer and closer. We musta hit it. I heard a pretty big thump. Too bad you missed it."

St. Louis

Bang! Bang! Crack!

"John? John? You awake?"

Crack! Crack!

"For about an hour. So, Rance, when are we getting up?"

Blang! Bzzzzzzzz! Crack!

"Up? Jesus H ... Up? John, this may be a stupid question but did you notice a sign on the beach last night? Something that said ... oh, I dunno, maybe *No Trespassing,* or *Danger?*"

"It was dark."

Thud!

"What the fuck was that?"

"I dunno but I'll bet it's on a tripod."

"Any holes in the tent?"

Crack!

"So far so good."

"How far is the river?"

"Missouri River's on the left and the Mississippi's on the right."

"Which way?"

"Towards the sunrise."

"Where are we?"

"Shit, I dunno. Maybe Missouri. Couple of miles north of St. Louis."

"Did you feel that? The ground moved."

"John."

"What?"

"I have to pee."

"Me too."

Bang! Bang! Bang!

"We'll have to slither out of the tent and pee lying down."

"You slither first."

"Watch where you crawl! I was up during the night."

Crack! Bzzzzzzzzzzzz!

"Musta hit a branch."

"How stupid is this?"

"It was dark. Never mind, we coulda camped in front."

"At least they woulda seen us. Not back here in the trees. Stupid, stupid, stupid."

"Stupid … as in getting run over by a ship?"

"Or being in jail?"

"Or paddling over a dam?"

"That was not my fault! You were in front, Rance!"

"Or getting swamped?"

"Which time?"

"John, while you're out there slithering, wave your undies at them. If you can't get their attention maybe the smell will kill them."

"Why do you always tell stupid jokes?"

"Why do you always get us into shit?"

"There's two of us here. You're not on a free ride!"

Crack! Crack!

"Hey, who was the one who said 'That beach looks pretty good?' No wonder it was so empty. It's being shot at by the Seventh fucking Cavalry!"

THUD!

"That's it! Outta my way. I don't know what that was, but it weren't no .22."

"Be sure to tell those guys on the rifle range that those idiots camped behind the targets are goodwill ambassadors from Canada!"

The manager held a cup of coffee halfway to his mouth as we stood before him and told him our story.

"You're camped where?"

We had just spent the last half hour crawling on our bellies along a drainage ditch to the back of the office. Covered in mud, leaves, and twigs, we had introduced ourselves to the manager of the rifle range. He answered his first question by asking another one.

"You set up camp behind the targets?"

Most mornings on our voyage down the Mississippi we started the day with coffee. This particular morning, on the outskirts of St. Louis, we had woken up to a barrage of bullets. Having experienced both, I can say with a degree of certainty that being shot at wakes you up quicker than coffee.

"Didn't anybody see the top of the tent?"

"It's green and dirty, just like the trees behind it."

"And it's in the shadows."

Over the public address system, the manager announced a cease-fire order. Soon a group of men could be seen walking down the middle of the rifle range. They stood shaking their heads as we quickly packed our gear and shoved off into the current. We waved, they waved, we paddled. For all that had happened so far on this trip, it was just another day at the office.

Having been woken up by the sound of bullets cracking overhead, I was optimistic that the day would get better. We left Alton, at the junction of the Missouri and Mississippi, and paddled towards St. Louis. Just about everyone we talked to told us to paddle down Chain of Rocks Canal. There is a large set of rapids just south of the Chain of Rocks Bridge. If we missed the canal and stayed on the Mississippi River the rapids would really ruin our day.

The canal was straight and calm. The only waves were from passing tugboats.

"Pretty slow."

"Yeah, we need a bit more of a current or we're going to be here all day."

We passed through Lock and Dam No. 27 — the last set of locks

▼

on the Upper Mississippi. It was a milestone. As the gates opened, we both cheered. It was a cheer that caught in our throats. We immediately started to back-paddle, trying to stay in the quiet waters of the lock.

Before us was the Mississippi like we had never seen it. The river undulated, tumbled, and rolled like it knew it was finally free of the restrictions of the dams. I saw brown hills that I thought were islands disappear and reappear like the hump of a prehistoric serpent. Debris flowed along with us and in the distance a tree, caught in an eddy, flowed north against the river, then started a lazy twirl and finally broke free, sailing on to New Orleans.

"You wanted current!"

"I thought the rapids were up-river!"

"Watch out for that tug!"

"I'm paddling!"

"The waves are coming!"

"Holy ... watch out! Watch out!"

"What for?"

"Can't you see?"

"What?"

"It's a friggin water intake!"

"Turn around! Into the waves!"

"Why?"

"We'll be sucked in, that's why!"

"Sheeat!"

We didn't paddle the canoe, we aimed it. Passing tugs threw up monstrous waves that we surfed in terrified combat. Barely under control, I felt the canoe settle and get sluggish. We tried to maintain some sense of direction. We needed to bail the ever-deepening water out of the canoe, but we were on the verge of losing control. Paddling was our only chance. We paddled hard, heads down, back muscles straining, lips working.

Two fishing boats set out from shore and followed us, shouting encouragement. They flanked us, taking the brunt of the waves. With that momentary reprieve we were able to bail out the swimming pool at our feet. Without the timely help of those two strangers, the trip, and maybe our lives, would have ended right there.

We slowly edged towards the far shore. Once we were close enough to safety our silent saviours gave us a wave and roared back upstream. We nosed into a cement shoreline. Getting out of the canoe, I looked up, squinting into the sun. We were right under the St. Louis Arch.

We waited two hours for a newspaper reporter who never came. We spent the time drying out and John answered questions from a number of tourists. I sat staring out at the river, ignoring John and the tourists.

"Rick, that woman asked you a question and you just ignored her."

"John, I've been a lifeguard my whole fucking life. I've seen three drowned bodies. I know when I'm in deep shit. We're in deep shit, John. You fucking talk to her."

I got up and walked away. I walked as close as I could to the Arch and back. I wanted to touch something solid, stable, safe. I wanted to sit with my back to that Arch and feel the coolness of its walls. I stayed within the shadow of one of its legs. I no longer wanted to look at the river.

John was still holding court, but with a new set of tourists. I walked by the group and picked up my paddle. He hastily said his good-byes, and gave me a sidelong glance as he got into the canoe.

While we paddled away we dug out our camera and took a picture of each other. I managed a grimace because I knew my mother would eventually see the picture, but John never cracked a smile. He's honest.

We paddled two more hours and pulled into a sandbank below the Jefferson Memorial Bridge. There was a sewage outlet close by. Figured.

The Marine

We drifted with the current.

John and I rested on our paddles, drinking in the beauty of the early
morning haze that had fallen over the Mississippi. There was no
sound other than the *poink poink* of the water dripping from the
oars. Suddenly from the green woods a rapid *snap-snap-snap* shat-
tered the calm. We stopped paddling to figure out which direction
the sound came from. There it was again — closer this time, louder.
We tried to peer through the forest of trees and weeds to no avail.
After all our adventures I had developed a good set of antennae for
this river. I eyeballed the bank.

"See anything?" John spoke softly.

"Whoever it is, they're watching us."

Long minutes suspended themselves like a pull of taffy. We were
about to resume paddling when a man, dressed in a white dress
shirt and a black tie, emerged from the grey foliage. For a moment
we stared across the water at each other. I raised my paddle in mute
greeting. The man on shore waved in return. Nestled in the crook
of his left arm was an assault rifle.

"Mornin'," he shouted.

"Morning yourself. You always get dressed up for target practice?"

"On my way to work." He looked down at his shirt, tie, and rifle
and grinned.

"Must be a pretty tough job!" John shouted.

"I sell candies!"

We all laughed, the sound jangling across the water.

"Hey! There's a boat launch and a restaurant about twenty miles down, on the west side. What do you say I meet you guys there about four this afternoon? Buy you supper."

"Sure! We'll try to make it by then."

"You be there!" he barked, betraying his smiling face.

"Okay, we'll be there!"

We waved as the canoe slowly drifted downstream. After a moment's hesitation he raised his rifle in salute.

"Why did you promise to be there? We don't even know what's between here and there. It could take us two days to go twenty miles. You know that."

"John, the guy had a gun."

We paddled all day towards our destination with the enthusiasm of an appointment with a dentist. Although the day had turned out to be warmer than expected, the man's shirt was as white and crisp as it had been that morning. He stood out from the bored fishermen scattered around the fish and chip shack like an icicle in a coal chute. His twenty miles by road turned out to be only ten by river, so, even though we had reservations about meeting this unknown rifleman, we were early. The small restaurant emitted a warm, humid smell of fish, vinegar, river mud, grease, beer, and cigarettes.

We sat out on the balcony in the sun. The man's neatly clipped black hair framed a face that was right out of a high school yearbook, except for the wrinkles around his eyes. After the introductions, I asked the obvious.

"You military?"

"Marines. Just got out. I guess it shows," he said self-consciously.

"My old man was a drill sergeant and he ironed his shirts just like yours. You could cut yourself on the creases. That's how I knew. That and the fact that you were clear-cutting the forest with a rifle."

"Yeah, we heard you shooting for a good half hour," John said. "You were alone, weren't you? It was only you?"

He shrugged his shoulders.

"That's a nice spot down by the water. Nobody bugs me there."

"I guess not. Who's going to bother a guy blasting away with an assault rifle?"

"When I first went down there the cops came. But they were a couple of local guys I went to school with, so they've left me pretty much alone since then."

"You must be a pretty good shot by now," John said. "Are you planning to go into competition?"

The marine smiled a grimace.

"I can't sleep. When it gets so that sleeping pills don't work I go down to the river and shoot."

Then he drained a full beer, tipping the brown bottle back until it was empty. John and I looked at each other. John motioned a silent whistle. The marine smiled brightly as he plunked the empty bottle on the table.

"Then I go merrily off to work."

"What time do you get up in the morning?"

"Three ... sometimes four. I can't shoot until the sun is up because people get excited, and like you said, the sound does carry. But as soon as the sun is over the trees, I start shooting," he said as he grabbed another beer. "They can't complain. It's government property and I haven't killed anybody yet."

"You starting to wind down?" John asked.

"Yeah, it's been a tough day."

"No, I mean slowing down from shooting so much."

"Yeah, I'm running outta money for bullets."

"No, I mean ..."

"I know what you mean!" he snarled. His boyish face contorted, pain flashing in his eyes. Then, just as quickly, he regained his composure. His smile was engaging.

"Say, where you guys camped?"

"Well, we were going to drink ourselves shit-faced and then camp on that island over there."

"Yeah, nobody would bug us out in the middle of the river."

"Well, why don't you stay at my place? I got plenty of room, besides it's gonna rain."

"Your wife won't mind?"

He stared at us blankly.

"She's gone."

The two of us looked at each other. The marine spoke up.

"C'mon. It's a big, empty house, and I got plenty of beer."

That decided it. It took a couple of hours of sculling but by nightfall our boat was overturned in front of his house. Soon the smell of fish and onions filled the hollow house, our voices echoing off the walls of the near-deserted rooms.

Other than a few kitchen mats, the place was barren. The only thing close to furniture was a brand new assault rifle leaning against the wall in the corner.

"I like what you've done with the place," John said.

The marine looked around the room with a faint smile.

The three of us sipped beer as we leaned against the fishing gear stacked around the living room. He drank three beers to every one of ours. The glow of the one lightbulb made the room stark. One after another, brilliant flies, caught in the light, would beat themselves to death against the bulb and fall to the floor. Slowly the talk turned to where we didn't want it to go. He started talking about Vietnam.

As lightning flickered across the horizon, he started rambling. Like spectators at a horrible accident we heard the screams, smelled the fear, sweat, and blood and were powerless. While the storm slowly built, he spoke of the smell of cordite, of the dead that were once his friends. He talked of fat rats and ants feeding on the dead, the red mud under his fingernails, and the all-pervasive smell of decay. He talked of Khe Sanh, Hue, Saigon. He talked and talked and talked. He only looked up once, when the thunder drowned him out. His droning voice and visions held us prisoner. As he slowly spun into his funnel of madness, our eyes sank into the black void of his.

It wasn't dawn when we left the house. It wasn't even pink in the east yet, but two of us couldn't sleep and the third was afraid to. On the horizon the night's storm moved on, soundless. We loaded up the boat at the water's edge and, after a nod to the marine, shoved off. The river took a slow, wide turn at that point so for an hour we hugged the shore, each of us lost in thought. It was easier to just drift, let the river make the decisions. After a time we started to row again, softly, like we didn't want to hurt the river. We stopped to watch the sunrise. All you could hear was the *poink poink* of the water dripping from the oars.

Ol' Man River

When people talk about Ol' Man River, they picture a kindly, old Mark Twain-type southern gentleman dressed in a tan suit, a little frayed at the edges, long silvery hair, and an ever-present stogie. To me, Ol' Man's a lot more like a mafia don who waves his hand and everybody shuts up. Once you've seen a barge the size of six tennis courts jerk sideways in a crosscurrent, then you know exactly what it means to be in the embrace of the Mississippi. "The Father of Waters" holds all those that sail upon him in his arms, but it ain't no cuddle.

South of St. Louis, the Mississippi flows like braided rope, its strands weaving, twirling, and twisting, scouring the riverbed, eating away at its banks. It constantly changes course and channels. It's gentle when you paddle with the current — sometimes you can't even tell it's moving. But try paddling against it. Then it reveals its true power. It's so deep there was a Second World War navy frigate moored in the shadow of the St. Louis Arch, smack in the middle of the United States. Here, the Mississippi, now carrying the contents of the Missouri, is too large to dam, the muddy banks along its edges susceptible to its whim.

The further south you go, the more you discover that being carried on the river is a physical sensation. You smell the salt from the ocean mixed with thick vegetation. The humidity coats you, and even though the temperature is in the sixties, until you reach the delta, you never really feel warm. Out of the sun, you shiver.

There is a strip of forest that follows the banks of the Mississippi all the way to the Gulf of Mexico. Occasionally, the bank is a moonscape with only the stubs of the giant trees remaining. With the exception of cities like Memphis, Natchez, and Baton Rouge, days would go by when we paddled through virtually the same forest explorers would have seen hundreds of years ago.

At dawn, the blurred light of the sun through the river mist would reveal trees with their great limbs bowed to the water in an act of supplication. Draperies of hanging moss recalled congregations of gaunt old men dressed in ragged prayer shawls. The muffled sound of water traffic would waver through the morning fog. The morning light would find us hunched over our coffee, shivering in our still-damp clothes, listening, smelling, and feeling Ol' Man River.

Diary Shakes

November 10, 1969

We almost quit today. We started out in a fog and spent all morning staring into the gloom. The current whipped us along at a good seven miles an hour. After two close calls with barges we arrived at Ste. Genevieve. After shopping for bread and milk we got back into the canoe. The wind had picked up from the south, kicking up waves which made it impossible to boat safely. My nerves are shot. We've had so many close calls in the previous few days that I don't want to get up in the morning any more. When I get out of the canoe for lunch or a break, I find it very hard to force myself back into it. I'm afraid all the time. We landed on a rocky shore where we made camp for the night without the tent, choosing instead to sleep under plastic and the canoe. John said I kept on muttering 'No, no ...' in my sleep.

November 12, 1969

Woke up at six. I didn't want to get in the canoe again so John and I had this huge fight about that. I was acting like a kid and I knew it but I couldn't seem to control my fear any longer. If I could meet each situation with time to react I would be alright. But we have had one close call after another. We had to paddle like hell to get out of the way of a barge, only to find we were headed for an eddy. So we'd shout and scream at each other and reverse our course into the waves and finally manage to get clear of that. This sort of thing happens every day. It isn't the exciting exception but the miserable rule. We keep right on plugging because to stop means to quit. I can't stop shaking. One of the things that gets me is that I spent every summer of high school as a lifeguard. I'm a really strong swimmer, and I have a healthy respect for the water. I keep my lifejacket tied to me. John, who has no fear of the water, lost his.

A Bottle of Rum

"This is too good for them, John."
"Who?"

"The Americans. Do you realize that nobody comes here? Nobody. And we're fifty miles away from a million people."

"Yeah. No tracks in the sand anywhere."

"They're out racing all over the country, paying big bucks for wilderness, and this place is just sitting here."

"Gawd, this is nice."

"A nice big fire. No bugs. Rum."

"You cold, Rance? You're shivering."

"Look at the stars."

"I haven't seen that many since we left home."

"Not a cloud in the sky."

"What's that constellation?"

"Well, there's the Big Dipper, the Little Dipper, and a whole bunch of stars."

"In other words ..."

"Okay, smart guy, you tell me."

"Well there's Orion, and that 'W' is Cassiopeia, and ..."

"And?"

"And a whole bunch of other stars."

"How are we going to navigate when nobody knows how to read the stars?"

"It's a river, stupid."

"Don't call me stupid. I have the rum."

"And a fine young man you are too."

"Hold your cup steady, you smooth-talking bastard. All we need now is one of them there double-breasted mattress thrashers."

"Yeah, right. Like women are just itching to get into your stinky underwear."

"Speak for yourself. I changed."

"What month?"

"I think the reason nobody comes here is because it floods every spring."

"It's funny."

"What's funny."

"We can paddle for days and not see another person."

"In the middle of America and nobody knows we're here."

"A thousand-mile-long strip of virgin forest."

"Ah, virgins."

"Like you."

"Some more rum? Hold your hands steady, for Pete's sake."

"Something I been meaning to ask."

"Shoot."

"I know why I came on this trip but why did you?"

"I dunno, but when I go away on a trip one of the things I find is me."

"Well, I'm here for the Hollywood lifestyle."

"And the entourage. No seriously, why did you come on this trip?"

"Seriously?"

"Seriously."

"I just didn't want to spend another night hanging around the pool hall. All the drinking ... speaking of which ..."

"Rum?"

"You know, you get out of the cities and the States are really beautiful."

"It's too good for them."

"You said that already, Rance."

"You always take great joy in reminding me."

"Let's send Nixon a letter telling him we want it back."

"Dear Dick ... all is forgiven."

"Know what? We stay in that boat, we're gonna die. The boat's too small."

"I know."

"I mean, how many fucking close calls have we had?"

"I never dreamed that the river could be so big."

"It's like a whole lake going south at five miles an hour."

"We've had so many close calls. It's getting so that I don't want to get up in the morning."

"You scream in your sleep."

"Surprise, surprise. We narrowly miss one hazard and practically fall into the next. We're not paddling, we're just dodging shit. I can't stop shaking. Look! Look at my hands!"

"Rum's gone. You know we gotta get back in the boat. We can't quit. We got all those newspapers, and our parents ..."

"You think I don't know that?"

"I know. I know."

"You think I don't see their faces?"

"I know."

"I just can't stop shaking."

On a Yacht

It had rained so hard for so long,
if he had been in Missouri that week, Noah would have been
nervous. The storm had scooped up the top inch of the Gulf of
Mexico and roared through, dumping it on an arc all the way to
Canada. It didn't rain so much as pound. We stood under the over-
hang of a marina in Cape Girardeau and wondered not when but
if the rain would stop. Slowly, the grey, ragged curtains of what
was left of the low pressure system moved north, spitting debris.
The deluge had stripped the trees, leaving the riverbanks naked
and ugly.

A shaft of sunlight broke through the clouds. Like an arctic tern
after a storm, a pure white yacht silently coasted through the sunbeam towards the dock.

An old man on the boat threw new nylon ropes to John and me
and we tied them to the old galvanized cocks. The man busied himself setting the bumpers between the yacht and the dock. When he
was finished, he joined us. Spanking our hands away from the ropes,
he reattached them to the dock. The yacht's engines revved and then
with a final, deep blubber, went silent. He knelt to tie and then re-tie
the ropes. John and I exchanged glances. The sunbeam fizzled out
on the far Illinois shore.

There were two men on the boat — the owner and a younger
man, Phil, who had been hired to captain it from the Great Lakes
to its home port of Boca Raton in Florida. Over a quick coffee in
the marina restaurant, Phil told us about the years he had worked

servicing and delivering yachts to countries throughout the world. He told us that the owner had bought this yacht over a year ago, and in that time had been on it six weeks. Our conversation stopped when the older man appeared at the marina door and brusquely ordered his employee to clean the master cabin. Phil's jaw clenched.

It was late in the season and getting colder, so John and I and the two from the yacht were the only people in the marina restaurant for supper. We sat together because it would have been rude to sit apart. John seemed to be impervious to the old man's abrupt manner. I never looked directly at him — he ate with his mouth open.

Halfway through the supper, a tall, elderly woman walked over to our table carrying one of those small beady-eyed dogs, the type that shivers when it's not being carried and most of the time looks justifiably worried. She slid into the empty chair beside the old man. By way of introduction he nodded to her and then to us.

"My wife," he mumbled.

They seemed an odd pair. He hunched over his food like someone was going to steal it. She sat prim and straight, leaning away from him slightly. She would start a conversation and he would cut her off — not once, but several times.

"Today I saw the loveliest little — "

"How many miles could you make a day in that little boat of yours?"

"Mmmm. Taste that soup, it's got a peppery — "

"How much money you spent on this trip so far?"

"Feel my hands honey, they're freez — "

"I was well on my way to my first million when I was your age."

Watching them together I had a vision of a guard dog chained to a tree.

Because the hurricane had thrown so much debris in the river, Phil suggested he needed extra hands to ward off logs. The marina staff told us that the stretch by Cairo, Illinois, was full of crosscurrents and eddies, and was always congested with barge traffic. John and I had experienced one too many close calls, so I really wanted a break. The older man mulled it over. By the end of the dinner, for better or worse, we were the crew.

At dawn the next day, the old man was eager to get away. He hustled his wife and the dog off the boat and then revved the two motors. I stood winding rope on the front deck as Phil passed.

"Phil, what gives with the wife? Isn't she coming?"

He smiled.

"The dog shit on the carpet once. So now he makes his wife and the dog get off the boat every morning and drive a rental to the next stop."

I stood there with my rope half-coiled, shaking my head. Phil motioned John to come over to where we stood.

"Watch yourself. I'll be down in the engine room for a bit, but the old man is chomping to get going and he wants to steer. It could get … interesting."

John and I stood on the front deck with long hooks ready. We couldn't hear the rumble of the motors, all we heard was the gurgle of the water under the bow. As we slowly entered the channel, we noticed debris everywhere. A marker buoy was dead ahead.

"Watch out for the marker buoy. Watch out for the marker buoy. Watch out for the marker buoy. WATCH OUT! WATCH OUT!"

Thump … thump … thump … "For the marker buoy."

The buoy spun astern with a new semicircle of white paint flashing in the cold morning sunlight.

By now we were in the middle of the channel of the south-flowing Mississippi. Unfortunately, we were headed east. We were on a collision course with the State of Illinois. The old helmsman glowered at the line of trees approaching at ten knots an hour, daring them out of the way.

We had about thirty seconds before we would be deep into the woods of a fast-approaching riverbank. John and I raced to the bow as if our presence would ward off the coming crash. John ran back to the cabin.

"Sunken log dead ahead! Turn hard right!"

The old guy listened to John and turned the wheel. And turned it, and turned it, and turned it. Slowly we spun around until we were rumbling at ten knots back towards the State of Missouri. I jumped into the cabin.

"Sandbank dead ahead. Turn left."

The wheel once again turned and turned and turned.

"Okay, stop."

The boat stopped. The owner stopped. Everything stopped. Steering wheel, engines, rudder, everything stopped. We silently drifted in the current, facing Missouri. Through the windscreen the old man looked at us and we at him. Then John and I looked at each other.

"Missouri. That's the Show Me State isn't it?" I asked John.

"Yep."

By this time, Phil had emerged from below wondering why the engines had stopped.

John and I stood on the foredeck as the yacht drifted aimlessly down the centre of the channel. A barge worked its way up the Illinois side. We stood at the railing and watched it labour against the current and winds, waves slapping its bow. It gave a loud blast of its horn, too loud for something that far downwind. A shadow moved into my peripheral vision on the right. Like a couple of metronomes, John and I turned and together looked up at another barge towering over us.

"Barge!" we yelled.

The owner looked through the glass, dumbstruck.

"Two barges!" We spread our arms and pointed east and west. Phil quickly grabbed the wheel, giving it half a turn. The owner shot a cruel look but allowed him to steer the boat out of harm's way. Two walls of red steel passed us, one going north, the other going south. A rich man's toy bobbed in the middle. We stood and watched the barges pass.

"You know, John, this guy doesn't have an ounce of common sense, no sense of direction, and you know what?

"What."

"He's an asshole."

"He's a millionaire — he must be doing something right."

"We're supposed to let things slide because he's got money? He had an anus replacement and the anus rejected him."

"Ah say."

John and I turned and looked at Phil.

"Ah say."

We stared some more.

"Ah, ah say."

We walked over to where Phil stood, big grins on our faces.

"Nobody ever said that to us before."

"Sorry?"

"Ah say. Nobody's ever said 'ah say' to us," John chuckled.

I turned to John and said, "That's the polite form for 'Hey you.'"

"If you want to try your hand at steering, the owner is going below."

Once Phil and John started steering, things became quiet. The steady thump of the motors and bright sunlight in the cabin made for comfortable lounging. We passed a major milestone on our trip when we motored past Cairo, where the Ohio River meets the Mississippi. Phil pronounced it *kay-row*.

John and I watched the debris, the waves, the eddies, and the barges. We glanced back at our canoe, safe and sound on the deck. I sat and watched the shore change from Illinois to Kentucky. I pulled out my journal and started to write.

Abruptly the owner came into the cabin, surveying the scenery and crew as he rubbed his eyes. His gaze fell on me.

"What are you writing?"

"My journal. It's the story of the trip."

He held out his hand. It wasn't a request. I hesitated. John and Phil quickly looked away. I handed my journal over. Except for the hum of the motors and the static on the radio, it was quiet. The owner nestled into the captain's chair as John stood steering the yacht. The sun streamed in, falling on the pages as I fixed my eyes on the horizon. When he finished he handed it back. He smirked and repeated the last line he'd read: "Oh, to be home safe."

I took it and put it back in my knapsack under a deep pile of clothes.

We tied up to a dock before sunset. There were better marinas further south, but the owner insisted we tie up there. It was open to every north wind and current — even the locals never used it. Every passing barge pushed the yacht into the dock.

In the middle of the night the boat began to shake as the wind picked up. Phil got up and looked out the window at a snow squall that had settled in. John and I stood shivering beside him. The one streetlight at the end of the dock revealed a swirling mess of snow. Waves slapped waves as the yacht slapped the dock.

"We need to get off here. We're too open. I'll look around."

We threw on our clothes as the captain started the motors to warm them up. As soon as they fired, the dog in the owner's cabin started yapping, which prompted the owner to start yapping at his wife.

"The wind is squeezing the boat into the dock," Phil said. "If we stay here, we'll be firewood. You two push the boat away from the dock and I'll back it up. Be sure to hold on!"

Waves smacked the north side of the yacht, sending ice and spray whipping over the top, drenching John and me. We strained against the side of the hull as the bumpers groaned and burped. They were squeezed so tight I wondered why they didn't explode into a thousand shards. One by one all the ropes were untied and thrown aboard the boat.

Phil gunned the twin motors as the yacht laboured against the bumpers on the dock. John and I strained as each pulse of a wave pushed against our efforts. The boat began to move, and John jumped aboard as he reached the dock's end. I had my hand on the railing and gave one final push off the dock, but slipped on its wet surface. The boat dragged me over the water. I hung over the side, my feet trailing in the water. John saw my hands on the railing and, giving a shout, ran towards me. Just as he reached me I was able to get a knee over the railing. We both pulled me up and sprawled on the slick deck.

"I'm getting off tomorrow, John. I'll take my chances in the canoe."

Arkansas River

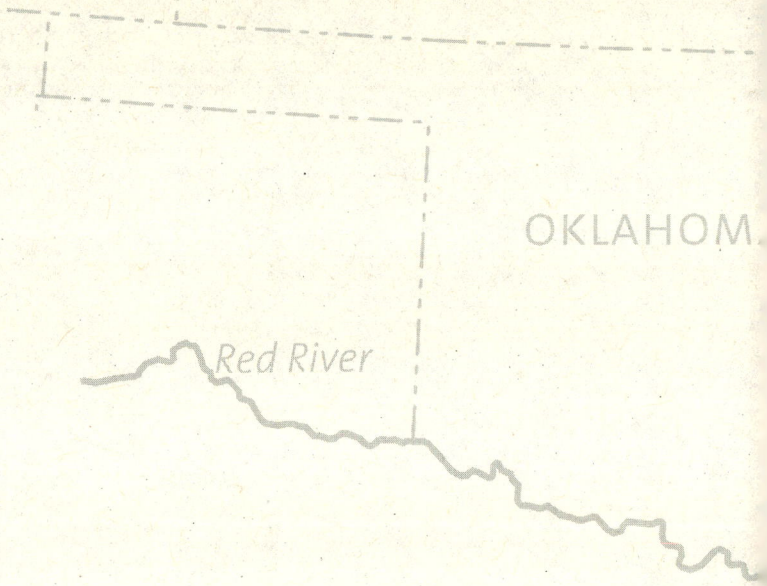

OKLAHOM.

Red River

TEXAS

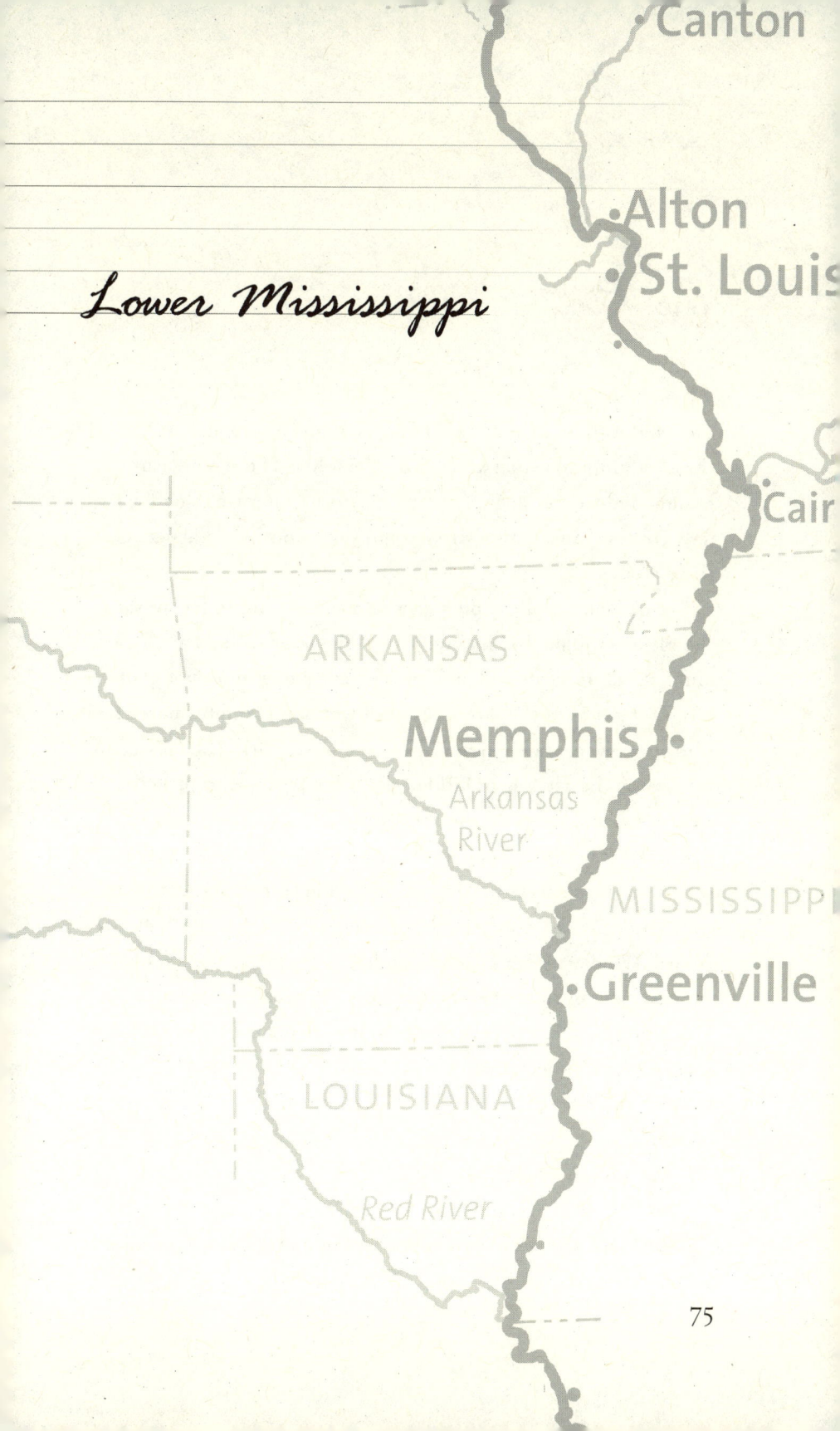

Lower Mississippi

Canton

•Alton
•St. Louis

•Cair

ARKANSAS

Memphis•

Arkansas
River

MISSISSIPPI

•Greenville

LOUISIANA

Red River

The Riot

Memphis.

The cold wall of air that swept across western Canada and through Montana soon arrived in Memphis. The temperature plummeted twenty degrees overnight. It was a crisp, cloudless day. On the bank of the Mississippi, John and I sat staring across the water.

We needed supplies and a general cleanup, but today we sat in the bleak sunlight and marked time. The river washed at our feet and behind us, scattered and knurled trees dug into the top of the levee. The tops of the buildings of downtown Memphis peered out over that levee, which muted the noise of the city. The only sound for us was the rattling of fall leaves in the trees. John picked up a small rock and threw it into the river.

On the other side of the levee, just a block away from where we sat, other people were picking up rocks and throwing them. They were throwing their rocks at the Memphis Police and the National Guard. Windows were smashed, buildings burned, people screamed. In November of 1969 in Memphis, riots were taking place over Vietnam. Lives, businesses, and homes were being destroyed. John reached for another pebble.

"Can you hear anything?"

"No."

"Wanna take a look?"

"No."

John and I were alone, our canoe loaded, our paddles at our side.

A letter of introduction from our city's mayor to the mayor of Memphis lay in the bottom of a knapsack, abandoned.

"John?"

"What."

"Ever get the feeling that people become like the land they live on?"

"How so?"

"Well, up north the Inuits are built like the trees, small and close to the ground. Around here, where the hunting was good, the Indians are tall, taller than the first white man."

"So, Rance, where are you going with this?"

"I think that the Mississippi is like America."

"Whoo, boy."

"No. Take a look at it."

"You noticed how much these Americans love their country?"

"Noticed? It's a friggin religion."

"It's like they compete to see who can love their country the most."

"I guess that's the difference between Canada and the States."

"How so?"

"They were born US citizens and we were born British subjects."

"So how's that make a difference?"

"Well, if you're a citizen you have to do something about it. You have responsibility. The whole damned place depends on you. But if you're a subject you don't have to do anything. You just are. Just obey the laws and shut up."

"Where'd you hear that?"

"History class."

"Figures."

"But it's true. These poor bastards have it pounded in that it's up to each of them to make the place better."

"And we Canadians wait for someone to tell us what to do. Is that what you're saying?"

"Well ..."

"If you feel that way, why don't you move to the States?"

"Because I'm not American!"

"Jeesuz, why don't you go watch the riot."

"Lookit, I think we got the best country in the world. But we define ourselves by saying we're not somebody."

"Well, we're not."

A cat poked its head out of a garbage drum, looked around, then slithered down its side. John tossed a rock in its general direction. The November wind picked up some leaves and trash and twirled them over the levee. We sat in silence, our backs to the country shredding its soul, throwing pebbles.

"You ever get the feeling we're pimping off the place?"

"You think too much."

"That's the trouble. I don't ... we don't ... think about Canada at all. We don't feel about the country one way or another. It's just ... there. We don't deserve what we got. And one day we're gonna wake up and we'll have given the place away. Nobody took it. We just gave the friggin country away. Piece by piece."

"Bloody Americans."

"Bloody Canadians. The Yanks have this taste for wide open spaces. And we got lots of that. We're just handing it to them. And you know why?"

"Why?"

"Because we don't give a shit."

"You don't know what you got 'til it's gone."

"Paved paradise, put up a parking lot."

"Maybe. Everybody's got an American friend, but nobody likes America."

"I like Americans. Well, most Americans."

"Shit, I even got cousins that are American."

"Is that the one in LA that was in the Amateur Strip?"

"I told you, John, it was a dare."

"I'd like to meet her."

"Nice tits."

"I'm sure glad I'm Canadian."

"Everybody likes us."

"We're harmless."

"Yeah, the foreign policy of Canada is 'Please ignore us.'"

"Rance, let's go watch the riot."

"Naw. Let's throw some more stones. Where's that cat?"

Green Waves and Dams

"Is it ever quiet."

We stopped momentarily, our hands resting on paddles held parallel to the river. The canoe, our world, a tiny chip of red suspended between the Mississippi and the cool Louisiana air.

Our ears rang with silence. The odd *slurp* of the paddles was our only conversation. A water boil from some deep obstruction blossomed in front of us. The canoe's bow dug into the swelling brown muffin. We slowed, then catching the outer rim of the boil, exited with a flourish.

The Louisiana shore, facing the morning sun, was pale green. There were many gaps and notches in the forest along the bank. The river and rich soil had created and nurtured great oak trees. Over time, the river had ripped away the trees' branches and thrown up mud and debris across their trunks — a violent disfigurement. In its final act of destruction, it undercut the soil the trees stood on. They stooped, genuflected, then collapsed into the river, joining countless others in an eternal procession to the Gulf.

The Mississippi shore, in the morning shadows, was dark, solid, grey. Entrails of fog hung along the bank, blurring the line between river and mud. The trees grew infrequently, like a gap-toothed saw. The early sun splayed through fog wisps, illuminating the tops of trees, hiding the bank.

We approached a bend in the river, one of a thousand or more that we would pass by during this segment of our trip. Through the trees and over the bank, we glimpsed the river downstream. It doubled back

▼

on itself, swinging east, then west. We were coasting along at a slow walk. Out in the middle of the river we sat motionless, enjoying the momentary warmth of the sun.

"What's that building over there?"

"Where?"

"Over there. Mississippi side."

"Where?"

"Through the trees. An apartment block."

"White?"

"Yeah."

"Dunno. Could be a weather station."

"Coast Guard."

We resumed paddling, the warmth of the morning's sun a welcome relief.

"That's funny."

"What's funny?"

"That apartment block looks like it's following us."

"Yeah, it does."

We stopped paddling and stared at the building as it ghosted through the Mississippi forest. It cleared a tangle of trees, an American flag fluttering high atop it. A ship's foghorn sounded.

"Oh, fuck."

"Not again! Not now! No. No. We're getting so close!"

"Paddle!"

"Which way?"

"Either way!"

"Mississippi side!"

"Hard! Go! Go!"

We laboured to make the shore as the ship's bow rounded the bend. It cruised along comfortably, pushing a bow wave — a handle-bar moustache. It swung around, pointing directly at us and our pounding hearts. We could see both sides of the moustache.

The river bank rushed by as we raced towards it. Half-submerged rock dams, built to control the river's flow, reached granite fingers out towards our flimsy craft. An eddy spun us around like a leaf in a gutter. Sometimes we missed rocks by inches. Sometimes we felt the scrape of granite furrowing fibreglass. The ship came steadily on.

A single tiny figure stood on the deck. A balding man with aviator sunglasses looked down at us and we at him. There were no waves, no greetings, no gestures of friendship.

"We're gonna miss it!"

"No. Look!"

In front of the bow, in front of the green, curling moustache, the water squeezed, rising to meet the ship. Once past the bow it collapsed in a trough, creating a mighty wave.

"Holy shit!"

The long green mound came towards us. Parts of the wave fell over on itself. Where the water had broken, cream-coloured lines of foam trailed. The wave splashed the shore, sucking back logs and debris. We rose, higher than we had ever been. Then we fell, as if over a waterfall. Walls of water surrounded us. In the bottom of the trough, we could see the tops of trees racing by.

The ship smacked past us, the roar of its engines ricocheting off the water and the banks of the river. Frozen, we flattened our paddles, using them as outriggers. Several more times the canoe rose and fell, jostled by countervailing waves.

Slowly, the river smoothed. Bumpy after-waves gave way to water boils and the beginnings of wind waves. Lines of foam marked the passage of the ship. We pulled the paddles back and sat silent.

After a time John twitched.

"Did I mention how quiet it was?"

The Bandage

So this was what the tail end of a hurricane looked like
— Greenville, Mississippi. Hundreds of miles inland and the low pressure system still had lots of power. The rain came down in torrents, shutting out the noonday light. The tin roof of the wharf we had taken shelter under sang out from the assault of rain. Silver splashes on the river hid the trees crowding the bank. A streetlight above the wharf produced a dull yellow glow. The asphalt street extending from the door of the warehouse disappeared, melting into the grey before it reached the dim glow of a second streetlight.

"What's the time?"

John examined his wrist, and then, squinting, held his watch up to one of the lights.

"Noon," he replied, shaking his head. "Friggin noon."

Dark figures moved inside the warehouse. Shadows appeared and disappeared as they passed through small pools of light, carrying boxes, bundles. A forklift, trailing the scent of half-burnt propane, appeared, its sound stolen by the rain on the roof. The operator parked it and joined a group lounging on bales. They sat, some hunched over paper bags and lunch boxes, staring at us. John, unaware of the stares, left to make the phone call to our contact.

He was a small black man, about my age. He sat alone on a bale of heavy cloth trying to eat his lunch out of a wet bag. He wore a faded yellow shirt, and had an old, red handkerchief wrapped around his right hand. The rag wound around his hand was so thick that his fingers were covered to the first knuckle, but blood still oozed. He winced periodically as pain shot through his injury. He ran his tongue over his soft full lips as he stared out into the rain. His eyebrows knitted as he flexed his fingers.

Our knapsacks were along the wall, away from the spray of the downpour. At the bottom of one was a first-aid box that had seen little use since leaving Canada. I walked over and rummaged through one of the bags. The young man looked up as I approached. The red box with the white cross on it announced my intentions.

"I got this first-aid kit and I've been dying to use it," I said, trying to ease proud feelings.

"I'd be much obliged."

'I'd be much obliged.' I'd never heard that phrase spoken outside of a TV. 'I'd be much obliged.' Sounded like half-smoked cheroots, old magnolia trees, chicory coffee, and pungent sipping whiskey. It was a throwback to the plantations that used to dot this land.

I knelt in front of him and we both removed his makeshift bandage. His wound was a repulsive tear. Curled skin and muscle followed a jagged ditch down his palm's lifeline and exited his hand at the heel. He would never have a single, clear lifeline again. Blood oozed from the flaps of torn skin as I tried to clean the edges.

"What did you cut it on?"

"Wore."

"Sorry?"

"Wore, barb-wore."

The first-aid kit smelled antiseptic, professional. His eyes widened as I cleaned out the gash.

"'Slotta blood."

"Oh, it's not so bad," I lied. "A doctor once told me that if you take a small cup of blood and throw it around a white room it looks like an axe murder. The sight of blood always looks worse than it really is."

My mouth was filling with thick saliva. For a moment I felt like handing him the kit and letting him figure it out. I wrapped a white bandage over the wound.

"See, it's not so bad."

The bandage quickly turned pink.

"You'd better see a doctor when you have a chance."

We both knew that wasn't going to happen. This was the bandage he would keep on until he healed, or infection set in. I smiled brittle encouragement to the young man.

"Leroy, ya'll go on back to work."

The command from behind was said quietly, but with authority. The young man abruptly left the box he was sitting on, the untied edge of the bandage fluttering.

I gathered up the white gauze as the forklift operator stood staring at me. He was fat and sure of himself. This was his arena. I smiled. It didn't work. He had a twenty-pound weight advantage. But I knew and he knew that if the fight lasted more than a couple of minutes, I would have the advantage in stamina. I had just spent two months paddling a canoe, and looked it. Behind him, three of his co-workers sat in studied relaxation. So I wouldn't have a couple of minutes. Me, my gear, and the canoe were going to go back in the water.

"We can take care of our own."

"I just wanted to help."

"We can take care of our own."

I slowly wrapped what was left of the gauze, keeping an eye on the operator. He looked back at the three men lounging just inside the shadows. We were caught, he in front of his coworkers, me with my back to the river. He raised his voice over the thunder on the roof. "We take care of our own."

I smirked. That sentence seemed to be the extent of his repertoire. "I expected that."

He was deciding something. We both knew what he wanted. But people like him would wait until they were covered by night and smelt of cheap bourbon. He looked towards our gear.

"Hey Rance!"

"Yeah!" I shouted a little too loud.

"The publisher's out! But his wife's sending down a car to pick us up."
John laughed as he reached the wharf. The operator had vanished.

I gave John a briefing. We arranged to load our gear onto a friendly
sailboat that was moored in the small harbour. We were soaked and
thinking of abandoning the promotional junket when the car drove up.

We had initially made arrangements to meet the publisher of a
magazine in Greenville. He couldn't make it, so his wife graciously
agreed to meet us at their house. She sat with her ankles crossed
and petite hands clasped in her lap. Her translucent skin contrasted
with grey-flecked black hair held aloft by a thin, patrician neck.
Even though the day was warm, she wore a sweater and matching
pleated skirt that had not been bought at the local Piggly Wiggly.
She had an aristocratic confidence that bordered on languor.

Her eyes glanced to a hovering servant. The woman snapped to
the table. "Tea? I heard that we were to entertain a couple of young
Englishmen. So I ordered tea. I hope it makes you feel more at home."

"It's okay, ma'am, we drink both coffee and tea at home," John
said. "Chicory is an acquired taste."

"Well, we can get you anything you want. You're in the south now,
and we are known for our hospitality."

"How has your trip been so far, Mr. Van? Any complaints?"

"No, ma'am. Everybody's been really friendly."

"And you, Mr. Ranson? You've been awfully quiet."

"I'm okay. It's just that ..." John snapped me a look. "It's just that
we've been outside for the last two months and every time we get
into a warm house I fall asleep."

"Oh," she smiled, looking between John and me.

"Well if there is anything we can do for you, just ask. Because we
do take care of our own."

Bob

One day we paddled by a small white sailboat tied to a fisherman's dock. We waved to the owner, who turned out to be Bob. His white teeth shone as he raised a beer in our direction.

The next day, his small sailboat passed us. With music turned to well above the pain threshold, his angelic smile flashed as he raised a glass to our meeting. This got to be a pattern. John and I would grind out the miles and Bob would flit like a butterfly all over the river.

He was alternately our saviour and executioner. John and I would get into one jam or another and just when things looked the bleakest, along would come Bob putt-putting down the river in his sailboat and rescue us. Then we'd follow him into so much shit we'd have to leave town in an awful hurry.

Late one night, John and I had taken refuge in Bob's sailboat due to a rain storm of biblical proportion. He left us on our own while he made for a rendezvous with a barmaid. The lady in question was reported to have rather blurry moral standards. In fact, Bob had been told that Miss Barmaid was known as the town ten-speed. About two in the morning he came ricocheting onto the boat, and with as much breath as he could muster, shouted out, "C'mon, get up! We gotta go!" As the lines were cut and the motor started, Bob glanced frantically over his shoulder. Through the rain and trees flashes of headlights from several cars raced towards us. As we rounded the buoy and headed straight out into the middle of the shipping lanes, we heard the shouts.

"How was I to know the bartender was her husband?" Bob panted, crumpled on the floor of the cockpit, chest heaving.

Now, Bob liked to drink. He was a happy drunk, a boisterous drunk, the loudest-in-the-bar drunk. One afternoon, as we sailed down the river, Bob was hugging the tiller of his sailboat, sipping bourbon and slowly getting mellow in the Louisiana sun. John and I slouched below listening to his singing. He rocketed all over the river looking at various things that captured his interest. He inspected a log, some oil drums, some buoys.

We relaxed below, reading but alert to Bob's whims. It was best to give him some space. Space was hard to get on a twenty-six-foot sailboat. Every so often one of us would put our book down, raise our head above the hatch, smile at Bob, inspect the river, and retreat to the warm cabin. The drunker Bob got, the more we inspected the river. After a time, I gave up the reading and stood in the hatchway.

"Shay! Give me that wood box."

"Where?"

"Down there, inna cupboard. Inna galley. Thash right."

I handed Bob the heavy box. He placed it on the seat beside the boat's tiller. I thought it was for a sextant. I was wrong. He slid off the top and pulled out the biggest, nickel-plated, pearl-handled handgun I had ever seen. I stared at it as a mouse watches a king cobra. Bob held it in the air, studying it.

I sat down beside and very close to John. He glanced first to my wide eyes then up to Bob. The gun glimmered in the sunlight.

BLANG! BLANG! BLANGBLANGBLANG!

With each shot, John and I flinched like we had straddled an electric fence. Bob was shooting everything. Logs, oil cans, garbage, river eddies. He shot anything that caught his attention. With each *BLANG* we cowered in our seats a little more.

Bob stopped shooting and gave us a long, bleary-eyed look. This was it. We were next on the list. He was going to shoot us and get away with it using the Texas Defence — 'They needed killin'.

"Shay, you guys wanna try?"

"Sure!"

"No!"

The difference between John and me was that when he said he was anti-gun, anti-violence and anti-war, he meant it. I, however, just mouthed all the correct phrases. In the end, I'd still rather be packing some serious heat. With a feeling akin to joy, I took the warm pistol from Bob. John sat below, sullen. I looked around for something to kill. Off in the distance, a log floated parallel to us. Taking steady aim, I squeezed the trigger. *BLANG!*

"Ouch! Ouch. Ouch. Ouch. Ouch!"

"Jesus!" John jumped up. "What happened?"

"Ouch! Ouch!"

"He shot Jeshush!"

"Ouch!"

"What?!"

"He shot Jeshush!"

"What?"

"Ouch! Ouch! Ouch!"

"Gun recoiled, hit him in the noshe. Shot that cloud. We call it shooting Jeshush!"

"I hurt my node!"

"You dumbass."

"Ouch. Did that cloud have a family?"

Shooting John

I think my friendship with John took a turn for the worse when I started shooting at him. Well, not exactly at him.

I really don't know what he was all pissed off about. I was shooting above his head, along the dock, and he was below in the bottom of the sailboat. John was perfectly okay if he kept his head down. All along the dock, you could hear him yelling, but every time he'd yelp I'd squeeze off another couple of rounds and pretty soon he'd stop. Legend has it that the outlaw Billy the Kid once shot a man for snoring. If that provocation was motive enough, he had nothing on us.

Try sleeping, eating, and staring at a guy's backside for three long months. After a while, our combined presence became like a constant toothache. Like a bad marriage we never made eye contact, avoided talking to each other, spoke in monosyllables when we had to, and passed the time within our own invisible walls. We didn't speak for so long that when a third party would talk to us it was a surprise that we had even retained the capacity to utter complete sentences. If I could have described the tension between us to a jury, no court in the land would have convicted either of us of murder.

That morning I had watched John eat. It was a slow, methodical, mechanical mastication. His eyes gazed straight ahead, semi-glazed. His jaw would go round and round and round. His head would have a slight tilt to it. If he could have bitten his toenail he would have chewed it the requisite ninety-nine times before he dared spit it out. His whole conscious being was concentrated on the pedestrian act of moving his jaw around and around and around.

After every second or third bite, he would straighten out his Fu Manchu moustache. It required two motions. The first was to stick his thumb and index finger under his nose and then follow the wispy moustache all the way down to either side of his chin. Then he would wipe his face by putting his hand over his mouth and dragging his jaw and bottom lip down to his collar, revealing his bottom front teeth — a real appealing look. He'd take a long, slow, full breath, then dive in for another bite. Then the jaw would start up again.

I watched him with a repelled fascination for a while before he realized that he was the object of serious clinical scrutiny.

"What?"

"You know my mom once said that if you love someone, you'd love them even if they were an axe murderer."

"Yeah? So?"

"If you don't love them, how they eat would drive you nuts."

"So?"

"So I've been watching you eat, and I'm afraid I'm going to have to kill you."

"Have you ever heard yourself eat an apple?" he asked. "You sound like a pony. Which reminds me, who took all the cookies?"

"Not me, but I'll sell you some."

"You better watch yourself, Rance, you're getting so fat they could lace you up and kick you down the field."

"I'm in shape."

"Yeah, round is a shape."

That was the longest conversation we had shared in a week.

It was a cold, clear autumn day. For once we were docked and out of the elements. Bob had taken pity on us and let us sleep on his boat. He was away for the day and had left us to our own devices. The dock in Natchez was a couple of miles from the city. Normally a busy place in the summertime, the landing was deserted in late November. It was a perfect day for target practice, for someone who had held a gun only once before.

Bang is too short and final to describe a bullet's sound in the cool still air. It's a ripping paper sound. The hum of violated air followed the bullet, and the echo returned in a kaleidoscope, bouncing off the bushes, slapping off the cement, cascading off the shallows of the Mississippi. The pistol gave me a feeling of power. I was surprised at its heft. It was smooth, sensual, and easy to use. Just a squeeze of the trigger. With a handgun you can kill anything you want.

There was a pile of discarded tins where the dock met the shore. I picked through the rusted containers and selected an aerosol paint can. It was different from the rest of the tins — it was new, barely used, worthy of shooting. I set it at the very end of the dock. There was nothing behind but Mississippi River and, two miles across, Louisiana. The boat in which John rested bobbed unseen below the dock. I lined up the can, taking great care. I relaxed, exhaled, and gently squeezed the trigger. The bullet was so far off it missed the river.

Second and third shot — same. I inched forward. Several shots later I moved a little closer. This was a lot harder than in the movies. So I lay down on the dock and rested the barrel on a piece of loose lumber.

The sound of the gun as it fired was immediately followed by the *psssssss* of the aerosol can voiding its contents — of black paint. The minirocket pinwheeled across the dock, spewing black mist over the entire area.

I stood up. There were freckles of black all over my face, every boat within twenty feet, on the dock, the signs, our canoe, our paddles, our drying underwear, our sleeping bags. The only thing that was clean was John.

The Call and the Girls

The Mississippi became a vast inland sea.
Ocean-going ships, barges, fishing smacks, and workboats, all grey and rusted, floated on its surface. Each boat tried to keep a straight course on water that flowed, curled, and tumbled over on itself. An oil barge muscled past going against the current, its bow wave high and steady. The rest of the barge followed the wave low, almost hidden in the river, croc-like.

The city sat high on a bluff overlooking the east bank of the river. Down below, we came upon a small, man-made inlet partially hidden by a line of trees. Tying our canoe to the dock, our eyes looked beyond the wharf to a group of ramshackle buildings that hugged the cliff. In front ran an old road that rose steeply to a switchback, then eventually into town. Tall grass encroached on the crumbling asphalt. Flecks of yellow that once divided the road now marked the edge, where a collapse had occurred years before.

The buildings down at dock level were flat-roofed, flat-faced, and leaned into each other for support. At first glance they looked abandoned by everything but time. The only thing that distinguished them from other industrial storage buildings was the amount of neon that hung from their facades. In the fragile morning light the neon looked like decorations on a Christmas tree — in a dump.

The temperature on the dock was twenty degrees higher than the river. The walk up that steep road to the mayor's office promised to be a long, hot one.

"Let's find a phone," John said, motioning to one of the buildings.

It looked tired. But it looked like a tired restaurant, and even they have phones.

I bumped into John as he stopped just inside the door. Looking past his shoulder, I paused to let my eyes adjust to the light. I couldn't see to the back of the restaurant but I sensed wary eyes watching me. There was a thick black bar to the right of the door with a thick black man washing glasses. Behind him was a mirror partially obscured by bottles of spirits, some full, some almost empty. The mirror was clean to a certain point on the wall. Beyond the bartender's reach, it was caked with grime.

It was a small restaurant. Dark red walls held newspaper clippings arranged in a crooked line. One wall featured historical pictures of the restaurant half-submerged by the river during some past flood. Another held signed glamour photographs of pouting starlets in various stages of undress. The wood floor creaked when anyone walked on it. There were a couple of tables, and judging by the size and feel of the menu, small greasy meals could be had. Scattered around were a few overstuffed easy chairs, the type that sell cheap, feel cheap, and stay around way beyond their useful life. Two of those chairs were occupied by women. A third was busy wiping the tables. All three smoked. It looked like they had just opened up.

"We're closed," said the bartender.

"We just need to make a call," John said, looking down at the phone in front of us at the bar.

"We're closed. Come back inna hour," he repeated.

"It's just a local call."

"We're not open." There was finality in his tone. Everyone in the room heard.

The woman wiping the tables walked over to us. "I'm sorry but we've had one too many people calling long distance on this phone. Sorry, honey."

Her voice was as brittle as her body was fat. She was dressed in a yellow, sleeveless blouse that showed off her several layers of arm. It was going to be a long walk into town.

Almost as an afterthought I reached in my pocket and handed her the letter. I understood then and there why cities put big letterheads on all their correspondence. Her reaction changed even the air in the restaurant. There was silence as she looked it over. Her lips were moving. She looked up at us.

"All the way from Canada, eh?" she snorted and smirked.

I smiled.

"Who ya wanna phone?" she asked, handing the letter to the bartender.

"Well, we were supposed to talk to the mayor when we got in. So I guess we'll start with him."

"You go ahead." She jiggled towards the phone. "But don't be making any calls to Canada." She winked at the bartender who was reading the letter. His lips were moving.

John smiled at her as he reached for the phone. She walked over to the overstuffed women in their overstuffed chairs and gestured towards us.

John talked to secretaries, executive assistants, officials, and finally to the mayor, reminding him of his kind letter. After several cities and several officials, neither of us had much awe left for politicians.

I nodded to the two seated women. They smiled back. If they were patrons in for their morning coffee, they seemed to be quite comfortable and were making it a long break. The owner, I supposed she was the owner, must have told them about us because they smiled each time I looked in their direction. It felt strange but oddly comforting to be a minor celebrity. People smiled at you, like those nice ladies sitting there.

The older lady with the short jean skirt and too-tight black sweater gave me a long lingering smile. She looked at me in a way that was, well, almost forward. I knew that if I had my '56 Chevy and a case of beer with me, instead of smelly old John and the tent,

I could get lucky. The guys had told me that you could tell when a woman wanted it, though I never could. Maybe I was getting better at that sort of thing.

The younger woman with the hooked tooth also smiled at me. I nodded, then turned to look out the window. Glancing back, I noticed her still smiling at me. Damn, where's a motel when you need one. I shifted. Hardened river mud rustled as my pant legs rubbed together. As I leaned over the bar beside John, who was still on the phone, the accumulation of several days of sour gas erupted from under my shirt. I stole a look at the two ladies — they were still smiling. My ego wafted upward, following my smell. I looked at the photographs of the starlets on the wall. Two of the pictures looked familiar. I had never been that good at thinking games but I was pretty good at connect the dots. I quickly realized that the two smiling ladies in the crumbling chairs were also two of the leering actresses staring down at me from the wall. Then it dawned on me that they were not in the acting business. But they were in business.

I spun around as John was talking to the mayor.

"Tell him we'll meet him on the wharf! Not here! Tell him we'll meet him by the boat! By the boat! Not here!" I frantically whispered.

Annoyed, John covered the phone with his hand and turned to me in a dismissive manner, as though a mosquito was bothering him.

"Why?"

"Cuz this is a whorehouse!"

On this trip I'd seen John in jail. I'd seen John scared. I'd seen John sick and I'd seen John cry. I had never ever seen him speechless. He stood stock-still with the phone in one hand, his other hand on the bar, and an expression on his face like he had just been electrocuted. A buzzing sound came from the phone. John said something unintelligible into it and slammed it down.

In due time the mayor came down and picked us up. We apologized for getting his nice new car dirty and answered all his questions.

He looked to the empty wharf, up the deserted road, and then across to the building we had just vacated.

"Where did you phone from?" he asked.

John pointed north and I pointed south.

"A gas station."

"An office."

The mayor snorted. As we passed the bar, three faces pressed against the window. The ladies waved. The mayor waved back. John and I sank into the seats. He looked at us and chuckled all the way to his office.

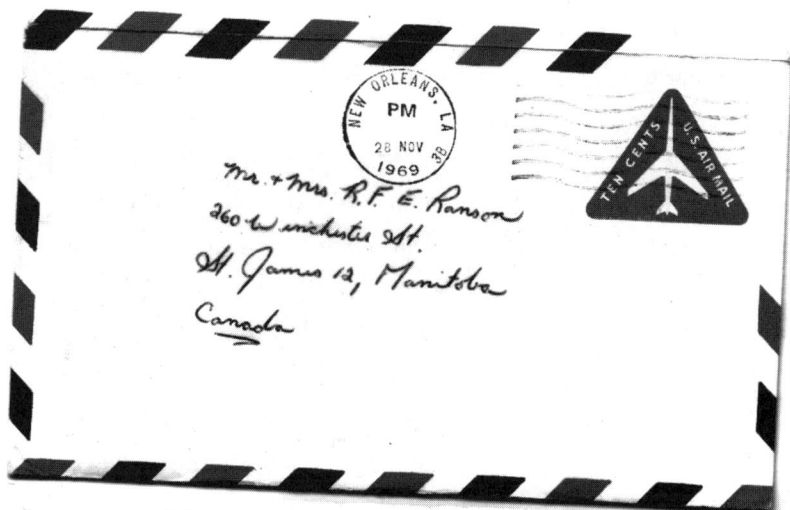

A Ship's Propeller

As I lay dozing, just on the edge of sleep, the last thing I expected to hear was screaming. Those screams and the *woof-woof-woof-woof* of a ship's propeller were almost the last things I ever heard.

All the way from St. Louis we had dodged forty-foot trees floating down the river, uprooted from the Mississippi's banks; leaves, roots, trunks, dirt, everything. Along with the trees, we shared the river with old lumber, garbage, sewage, and oil barrels, all headed south. We paddled beside logs that disappeared into whirlpools and, once released, shot skyward like spears. Barges loomed out of the morning fog, missing us by feet, and then quickly disappeared.

After Baton Rouge, we figured we had proved our point. We had paddled well over 2,000 miles and just wanted to get to the Big Easy alive. We hitchhiked a ride with Bob, lashing our canoe and considerable gear to the topside of his sailboat. Bob wanted to keep going well into the night to avoid the dangerous daytime congestion of river traffic. He thought there would be far fewer boats to contend with. New Orleans is the second busiest port in the United States. But the traffic wasn't any lighter at night, it was just harder to see.

There was no moon but both banks of the river twinkled with the lights of refineries, dockyards, and various other industries. We thought we could see all the traffic on the river because passing vessels were well-lit and would blot out the lights behind them on shore. This was true for activity to our port and starboard, but we were soon to realize that we had a huge blind spot to our stern.

Having finished my watch at the tiller, I was in the quarter berth trying to sleep. A quarter berth in a small sailboat is a glorified coffin, tucked under the stairs. To get into the bunk I'd slide into it much the same way as getting into a drawer at a morgue. John had replaced me at my post and Bob was slouched beside him in the cockpit. They were making lazy, disjointed conversation as I drifted off to sleep, the slow waves and droning motor gently lulling me.

I had the distinct impression of the boat lifting up and swinging sideways. That motion and the startled shouts of my friends slapped me awake. I wiggled out of my bed and landed barefoot on the floor, which heaved and fell away. Opening the hatch, I climbed into the cockpit. My eyes were first attracted to the lights of a refinery on our port side. Despite the violent rocking of the boat the lights seemed normal. Turning to starboard, I saw no lights at all. Just brownish black. Then a line of rusty welding passed by my face.

I was staring into the side of a ship. John turned the boat hard over. The ship passed only feet away, the rumbling *woof-woof-woof* of its propeller half out of the water filling our world. The waves it produced pushed us safely out of the way.

When you're young and stupid you figure you're immortal. With age hopefully comes wisdom. Wisdom to not travel at night, in a little sailboat, on one of the busiest waterways in the US. Whenever I think about what can happen to the foolhardy, I always remember the sight of a line of welding, and the sound of *woof-woof-woof-woof-woof.*

New Orleans

Ohio River

KENTUCKY

Cairo

TENNESSE

Memphis

Arkansas
River

MISSISSIPPI

Greenville

LOUISIANA

ALABAMA

Red River

Natchez

Lake
Pontchartrain

on Rouge

New Orleans

of Mexico

Arriving

We sailed into New Orleans unannounced
and ignored, just another piece of Mississippi flotsam sharing the
river with a steel line of massive container ships tied up to the wharfs.
Tugboats and barges, all business and speed, bullied the waters in
front, behind, and alongside us. We got the impression that industry
was very much more important than adventure, and if any little craft
got into trouble alongside the giant ships, it was on its own.

Late afternoon sunlight caught the tops of the waves and shone
off the windows of the warehouses that bordered the river. We were
so busy with the mechanics of sailing into the busy seaport that we
failed to notice the weight slowly lifting from our shoulders. It was
gone, but the bruise it had left from the burden of other people's
expectations kept us focussed on our vulnerability. Our eyes warily
watched the waves, the other vessels, and the wind and the currents,
right up to the last moment of the voyage.

The aromas in New Orleans are striking. Cajun cooking from
hundreds of small restaurants, boiled crawdads, baking bread,
magnolia trees, oil flares from the direction of Baton Rouge, and
the water — the thick, earthy Mississippi and the brackish Lake
Pontchartrain all mix with the pervasive humidity.

Later on in the evening, when we subconsciously started making
plans for the next day's voyage, it finally dawned on us that it was
over — no breaking camp, no packing of the tent and gear, no dodging
ships, debris, or waves from barges. That's when thoughts of survival
turned slowly to feelings of triumph.

We were sitting in a seedy New Orleans bar, having a beer and a store-bought sandwich, when I reached over and shook John's calloused hand. Together we mumbled congratulations and quickly resumed eating. Over the course of the meal John and I started to smile. And we kept on smiling.

"How do you feel?"

"Like I finally passed outta school."

"You sorry it's over?"

"Not in the least."

"Me neither."

"I'm tired, John."

"So am I."

"I don't mean physically."

"I know. You haven't told a sick joke in days."

"What is this? I joke therefore I am?"

"Drink your beer, Rance. Let's call it a day."

Both Winnipeg and New Orleans keep a worried eye on the rivers that slice through them. They try to keep them in their place, within their banks and levees. The rivers, though, have minds of their own — both cities have, on several occasions, been swamped by them. There's a fatalistic feeling in New Orleans and Winnipeg that digs to the core of their collective psyche, that one day the water will win.

A Farewell to Bob

On one of the last nights that he was in New Orleans, Bob treated us to an old-fashioned pub crawl. We were soon to go our separate ways — Bob to the Caribbean, and John and I back to Canada. This was goodbye.

We went to tourist bars, jazz bars, country and western bars, Cajun bars, longshoremen's bars, biker bars, bars that were beautiful, bars that stunk like a cat's litter box, and finally, just as the sun was coming up, we walked into a bar that wasn't in any tourist guidebook. It was the lowest of the low. The only thing going for it was that it was open. John, the most sober, took three steps in and four quick ones out. He got into the rental car, locked the door, and lay down in the back seat.

Bob, whose idea of sport was carrying a beer from one smoke-filled room to another, was grabbed by the arm and fired like a frisbee onto the dance floor by some hulk of ambiguous gender. After the dance, which can only be described as a cross between the twist and a Greco-Roman wrestling match, Bob rasped.

"A shim! It was a shim!"

"And you made a lovely couple too, Bob."

I think that was the closest he ever came to hitting me.

"Come on, we gotta go."

"What? Not going for best outta three, Bobby?"

"Don't you Bobby me!"

Before we left he put a dollar's worth of dimes into the jukebox. For ten dimes he got to select ten songs. He chose "Leaving on a Jet

Plane" — ten times over. Probably the only time that song has ever been used as a weapon.

The Media

"You want me to do the talking this time?"

"I'm better at it than you."

"No you're not, Rance, you're just continuous. You never stop."

"You always criticize."

"You never stop."

"I never liked you, John."

"Never stop."

"Shhh! Here he comes."

"How do you do. I'm Rick Ranson."

"And I'm John Van Landeghem."

"Hi, I'm from the *New Orleans Times Picayune*. I'd like to ask you a few questions and get a picture of you for Saturday's paper. I wrote down a list of questions on the way over."

"Shoot."

"Well, for starters, why did you go on this trip?"

"Partly to celebrate our province's centennial next year."

"Tell him about Huckleberry Finn."

"Okay, okay. John gets a chuckle out of this. It may sound corny, but I was really taken with Huckleberry Finn. Not so much the book as the idea of a voyage down the Mississippi. It started me thinking about a trip. It seemed affordable, and besides, the river that runs behind my house eventually links up to the Mississippi."

"I'd have to agree with Rick," John added, "but also what better thing to do, before getting on with the rest of your life, than go off on an adventure. And how hard could it be?"

"Yeah, how hard could it be?"

"Pretty hard, actually."

"Ya know? I just didn't want to spend another night hanging around the pool hall."

"How much gear do you have."

"About one hundred and fifty pounds in four knapsacks. We started off with everything but the kitchen sink. We had a radio, rifle, twelve changes of clothes, pots, pans, and a whole box of propaganda that the Centennial Corporation gave us."

"Yeah, some of their shit turned out to be inter-office memos."

"Memo paper?"

"Yeah. I guess they didn't believe we'd actually do this so when they heard we were shoving off they grabbed everything they could as they ran out the door."

"You want a Manitoba pin? We got a million of 'em."

"John, give him a non-rusty one."

"Here you go. Just don't wear it on a white shirt."

"So now we're down to a change of clothes, food for a week, a tent, a stove — that's about it. We could set up camp or break it in minutes."

"Where did you eat? In the canoe?"

"No, we stopped along the riverbank every two hours or so. It's funny, everybody asks that. It only takes us minutes to pull into the riverbank, get the stove going, and boil up some coffee. We'd make sandwiches and talk about the river, or anything."

"We didn't talk that much."

"You didn't talk?"

"What John means is, I talked, he listened."

"Who says I listened?"

"Go on."

"Well, if it was raining we'd stop under a bridge. If it was nice out we'd try to pick someplace scenic. We even had lunch on a sand-bar in the middle of the river. Sitting there having our sandwiches and waving at the boats as they went by. We really needed a break every couple hours. Paddling is boring, man!"

"Who did the cooking?"

"John. He comes from a family of bakers. He's good at it. I tried it for a day or two. It didn't work. So I cleaned up. I didn't mind."

"How far could you paddle in a day?"

"Dammed if I know. Somebody else asked us that, so we just took the length of the Red River from Winnipeg to Fargo, divided it by how many days it took to get there and came up with thirteen to fourteen miles a day."

"The Red River. That's not the one in Texas is it?"

"No."

"I didn't think so. You were paddling upstream on the Red River?"

"Yeah. We were paddling upstream going south."

"What Rick means is the Red flows north and the Mississippi flows south, so after we got on the Mississippi we were going downstream coming south."

"Who's on first?"

"Shaddap, Rance."

"Once we got on the Mississippi, north of Minneapolis, we averaged about twenty-five to thirty miles a day, but that was using a road map to calculate. South of Minneapolis there were mileage markers on the river so it was easier. South of St. Louis, we averaged forty to fifty miles a day."

"Once in Mississippi, I could see across the riverbank to where we had camped the night before. By the river we had gone ten miles, but as the crow flies we were still just a long walk from where we had slept. The Mississippi switches back and forth so much it goes east and west just as far as it goes north and south."

"Is there anything you would do differently?"

"The boat is way too small. We underestimated the size of the river below St. Louis. We were almost killed so many times we got to the point we didn't write the incidents down in our journals.

Almost getting run over by a barge ..."

"Or sucked down by an eddy."

"Almost being hit by a deadhead."

"Or going over a dam."

"Almost getting shot."

"Shot?"

"It was just target practice! Jeez, John, give it a rest!"

"We had so many experiences it was almost boring. Well, not boring, it was never boring, it became common. We were a leaf in a rain gutter. A sixteen-foot canoe is way too small to be on the Mississippi south of St. Louis."

"Shot?"

"Yeah, and I'd start the trip in Bemidji. The Red River's a drag. South of Winnipeg it's muddy, shallow, and this time of year full of branches."

"Tell me about getting shot."

"Somebody lent me a gun. I tried some target practice. John exaggerates."

"Okay. How are you going to get back to Canada? Are you going to paddle back?"

"You know, a lot of people ask that question."

"You already said that Rance."

"What?"

"A lot of people ask that question. You already said that."

"Mmm. As I was saying. John bought my half of the boat and is going to ship it back to Canada by truck. We'll fly back to Winnipeg."

"We can paddle at about five miles per hour, the river current is about four. That means that after ten hours of paddling we'll have gone, tops, ten miles. At that speed it would take us two days just to get out of New Orleans. Paddling back up north is not an option. People have done it, though not in this century."

"Would you ever do it again?"

"No. Why bother?"

"How did you get along with each other?"

"Well ..."

"Well ..."

"I see."

"When you consider that for the last three months we've been jammed together in an area a little bigger than a phone booth, we've done pretty well. We've eaten together, slept together, washed together, paddled together, been interviewed together ... well ... okay, okay, it's been hell."

"What was the worst part of the trip?"

"That was it. For the last two months we've been carrying around a real bad case of cabin fever."

"What was the best part of the trip?"

"The people."

"Yeah, we talk about the river but it's the people we met along the way that really made the trip. The funny, weird, touching stories that we heard. People are best at being, well, people."

"Yeah, people are the same all over the world."

"Thank you. That's all the questions I wrote down. I'll take a few pictures of you in your canoe. Look for the article in Saturday's Leisure Section. Thanks again."

"Well, that went really well. See what happens when you let me do the talking?"

"You'd better get that straight. Have we been gone two months or three?"

"It feels like ten friggin years. Why do you always criticize?"

"You always exaggerate."

"No I don't!"

"Yes you do!"

"Don't!"

"Do!"

The Honey Trap

There was that sweet girl in Winnipeg.

I carried her Mississippi-soaked picture all the way to New Orleans.
Then there was 'Rocky' — Roxanne from Minnesota who was such an
expert flirt that both John and I were convinced she only had eyes for
each of us. There was the young lass in Cape Girardeau who wanted
one of us to end our foolish trip and move in — a meeting with her
parents could be quickly arranged. I don't think she really cared if it
was John or me, either one would do, as long as whoever it was had
a pulse. And finally, at the very end of the voyage, there was Honey.

"Where can I get a good rare steak, José?"

Thin as a cadaver, José slouched in his greasy, old oak chair. He
balanced his tailbone on a felt pad that was tied to the chair's ribs.
He wore a thin black moustache, a concession to his Spanish blood.
His crisp Esso uniform, a testament to his hard-working wife, stood
out smooth against the wrinkles on his sun-battered neck. His fingers
were linked in his lap as his head swivelled from boulevard to canal
like a drunk tennis fan. He stopped searching for customers long
enough to idly straighten out the crease on his pant leg.

"Well there's the Man ... Mand ... Mandoleum Palace, shit, I
dunno what they call it. You know, that Chinese place down the way,
but they been closed down a couple of times."

"How come?"

"Cockroaches. People forget that this whole place was built on a
swamp. If you don't keep after them, you get cockroaches."

"Chinese steak. I don't think so. What about that place down there?"

"You don't want to go there," he warned me. "Do not go there."

José's gas station was at the Lake Pontchartrain end of a long New Orleans boulevard. Cars gassed up on the boulevard side while yachts fuelled up at his docks on the canal side. The car side was all business, so the occupants could get back to work. The yachts leisurely filled up before they ventured out across the lake, skirting the Gulf of Mexico to Mobile, Alabama, Fort Meyers, Florida, or even as far as the Keys.

The street was lined with boatyards and tired bars pimping off the traffic along the canal. The faded buildings and their even more faded neon signs petered out the closer to the lake they got. In the middle of the block, sandwiched between two boatyards, was a solitary squat building. It stood alone like the last picket on a fence after a hurricane. From José's garage it looked like it was either red or black. Whatever its original colour, it was now trying to switch to the other shade. In a city full of ornate structures, this one looked like someone had kicked over a tombstone.

"They got a sign that says steak dinner."

"That's for members only."

"It's a club?"

"You could say that," José smirked as the gas bell clanged.

The next day I walked past the building, furtively peering in its tinted windows. Every once in a while, a large black car would pull up to the door and men would get out. Club members having steaks. Sometimes they would stand and talk for a moment on the sidewalk. Just like us kids did in front of the pool hall back home.

I first saw her one afternoon after all the other businesses had closed. She materialized in front of the old building, her hair bouncing as she trotted across the boulevard towards Jose's. A carload of kids drew up to the gas pump, blocking her from view. I craned my neck and stared. Close up she wasn't as young as I had thought, but she wasn't that old, either.

"That's Honey," José said, rising to stand beside me.

"They got that right."

▼

"Just one of the perks of working around here."

"Perks," I sighed. There was a long pause as the two of us watched that perfect woman stride down the block away from us.

"Nice perks." There was another long pause.

"Watch yourself, José, you're leering at the woman I love."

"Last week she came in here driving her little yellow beetle and said those three words I love most."

"What was that?"

"Fill me up."

"So, José, how do I get to know her?"

José snapped a sharp look. All banter gone.

"You don't. Like I said, and I mean it, you don't want to go there."

Over the next three days I watched the block and made a point of being close to José's gas station around Honey's quitting time. Every afternoon she would walk the boulevard in the fading light towards her little yellow car. She always wore something summer-like, always luminous against the sleepy purple of a New Orleans winter. The second day she walked by, she gave me a cold once-over. On the fourth day, I marched right into the old building, without a thought of José's warning.

My reflection wavered in the plateglass window, the bell ringing as the door closed behind me.

The restaurant was spartan — a few tables placed haphazardly around the room and four uncomfortable nooks that hugged the perimeter. The tinted window had a diagonal crack in the corner where the tint had faded. The brightness of the street outside was a shock.

Honey was wiping the bar with a large white towel. I eased into a stool, trying to act nonchalant.

"The sign outside says steak dinner."

You could tell she worked out. There was definition to her body. The muscles in her tanned arms and legs were distinct.

"You a ballet dancer?"

She shrugged her shoulders. "Tried to be." She gave me a puzzled look.

"The way you walk. A girl I knew was a ballet dancer."

It wasn't much of a stretch to imagine Honey was still a dancer, but I'd bet she now danced with a pole.

She was about to say something when her eyes flashed to either side of me. I turned. Sitting to my right was a giant. He had black hair, black suit, black tie, black shoes, and a dark complexion. Seated to my left was the largest mouth-breather I'd ever seen. If we all stood up, I would have looked them both right in the nipples. My head swung back and forth. I said the first thing that came to mind.

"Hello."

"'Lo."

"'Lo. Where ya from?"

"From Canada, I'm staying on a boat in the marina."

"Yours?"

"No. I came down here by canoe."

"You came down the Mississippi by pirogue?"

"Canoe."

"Pirogue."

"What's a pirogue?"

"A canoe."

I took out the newspaper clipping, which I had brought to impress Honey. I thought it might save my ass from an imminent shit-kicking instead. Besides, as soon as the two mastodons showed up, she left the bar so fast the towel seemed to float.

The dark-suited man-mountain took the clipping and slowly read it. Then he smiled. I wish he hadn't done that.

"Don't go away. I'll be right back."

I looked at mouth-breather, still sitting beside me — he smiled. I wish he hadn't done that.

"I saw your canoe, at the gas station."

Thank God I just sold my half of the boat to John. Sorry, John.

"Dis is kind of a private club," mouth-breather said in a conspiratorial voice.

"Oh sorry, I didn't know," I lied. I stood to leave.

Mouth-breather put his hand on my arm. It was heavy.

"S'okay. S'okay. Looks like the Chief wants to talk to ya."

We were motioned to come behind a screened-off area. Four men sat at a large round table playing cards. Three of them wore black suits, the last man had a grey Polo shirt. The shirt must have been cut from a circus tent because the man it covered was easily three hundred pounds. I didn't think it was possible, but he made the first two guys look small. He introduced himself as Chief. He extended his hand. I watched as mine disappeared into a bread loaf with fingers.

"Dis you?" He pointed to the clipping.

"Yes. Me and my partner paddled from Winnipeg, Canada. Took us three months."

"Sit down. Sit down. Honey!" The screen shook. "Get this young man a drink!"

"Thanks. I was looking for a steak and your sign said …"

"Honey! Whatever he wants."

"So," he nudged the beer Honey set in front of me, "tell us some lies."

I had been answering variations of that question for the better part of three months so this part was easy. Once you get an audience laughing, you're in. So I started with a few quick stories to get everybody warmed up. Before long they were all smiling and laughing. Honey set a steak in front of me and I ate as I talked. I told them about the fog, the dam, the tugs, the ships, the camping, and the never-ending close escapes. One or two of them were following me and changed expressions whenever I did, so I knew they were hanging on every word. The Chief, well he had a half-smile. He asked questions while the others looked on. Where's home? Canadian? What did my father do? Brothers? What did they do? He was real interested.

Slowly, I wound down. Chief sat and looked at me the whole time with that half-smile. It started to get on my nerves. When I finished my meal, he walked me to the front door. For a large man he didn't come down on his heels hard. He walked light, like a boxer. Honey came with the bill and he grabbed it, putting it in his pocket. His huge hand surrounded mine once more and he smiled me out the door. I hadn't noticed how the steak tasted.

The next night José and I were at our usual spot. He watched the store and I watched the passing boats. I turned and noticed Honey approaching, the late afternoon sun at her back. She walked passed José and stood in front of my blinking eyes.

"I'm going downtown, want to come along?"

I sat there stunned. José sat there stunned. Honey looked back and forth between us, her head tilted a little.

"Well?"

"Sure," I croaked.

"Well, c'mon." She walked briskly towards her car.

My wide eyes met José's as I dutifully followed those undulating hips out the door.

Honey drove her beetle with the windows open and her hair fluttering in the wind. She was quiet. Most conversations are like tennis games — you talk, she talks, you talk, she talks, back and forth, back and forth. Unless you start talking and she doesn't say a word. So I tried to fill the emptiness with noise. I babbled away and she nodded. I imagined that, in the back of her mind, she was probably wondering what she was missing on TV. Such was the first hour of my date with Honey.

We had a light supper in a restaurant so old it was built when those uncouth settlers up the river were called *Les Amerique*. The hand-wrought balcony railings were older than Canada. Judging by the lineage of the clientele that sat beside us, not only were they miffed the Union had won the war, they were downright pissed Napoleon had sold out to the Yankees in the Louisiana Purchase.

A tottering old gentleman's slow nod to Honey brought a sharp reproof from his equally tottering wife. Honey tossed her head back and blew cigarette smoke towards the couple. She smiled her first smile of the night. It was actually more of a sneer. Something wasn't quite right.

She drew on her cigarette and watched me eat, "Finished? Let's walk."

I reached for the bill, but her hand beat me to it.

"It's been taken care of."

We walked down Royal Street and looked at the buildings, crossing the street to get a better view. All of a sudden, Honey became animated. She spoke of the people who had once lived there with such passion she brought them alive. A defeated confederate general eked out a living in this building. Yankee carpetbaggers gloried in his humiliation. While visiting France, the wife of the owner of this building was approached by Napoleon for her auburn hair. He wanted to make a wig for the Sultan of Turkey's harem. A wine merchant built that building over there, going broke and living the rest of his miserable life in abject poverty, his building in the hands of others. She spoke of them as though they were her relatives. She lived in a stage play of her own imagination, surrounded by shadowy bit players who haunted the French Quarter. Reliving the lives of the dead was the only time she showed interest in anything, other than pulling on her endless cigarettes. I started to think that she didn't have all her paddles in her pirogue.

We wandered Bourbon Street and bathed in the lights of that circus midway. Honey retreated into herself. She hurried, her high heels clicking on the pavement. There was a real hardness to her, evidenced by her treatment of the elderly couple earlier on, but she had a vulnerable charm when she escaped into the past lives of others.

"You ever watch *Gone With the Wind?*" I asked, on a hunch. It was like I had thrown a bucket of gasoline on a fire.

She erupted, going on and on about Scarlet O'Hara and Rhett Butler, and that poor Ashley and Tara — lovely, red-earthed Tara.

She gushed, she blossomed, she held my hand. I was right, Honey had seen it, she'd seen it twenty times. And Honey was as crazy as a shithouse rat.

We wandered down several alleyways as she gushed about Margaret Mitchell and all the characters in that book. She knew them all, referring to them by their first names. We ended up on a side street. There was a series of doors in a brick wall. No yards, no fences, just doors, with a lonely streetlight at the end. Honey unlocked the door to her sparse two-room apartment and let me in, talking all the while.

I turned in the hallway, and Honey wrapped her arms around me. Her soft, open mouth pressed down on mine.

There was a humid scent of light rain on tar from outside, and the smell of chicory coffee on Honey's breath. There was the fragrance of spicy jambalaya, and the sweet olive trees mixed with the bakery down the lane. Her eyes fluttered and a snarl came to her face when she did. Honey was a prefect child of New Orleans, living in memories, sweat-soaked, heavy with her animal funky scent and more than a little crazy.

She drove me back to the marina, all the way across the city from the Mississippi to Lake Pontchartrain, without uttering a word. Before I was fully out of her little yellow car, she pulled away.

"I don't want you hanging around here," José said.

"What I do?"

"Just go. If you're smart you'll keep on going."

José barred the garage door. Behind him, in the shade of the office, stood his employees and my former acquaintances, expressionless.

"Look, I don't know what it's like up in Canada but here, we don't talk to those people."

"Look, I'm sorry."

"Saying sorry is always too late." He looked right then left, then back at me.

"I seen this before. What's gonna happen now is they're going to ask you for a favour, deliver a letter or something. You know you can't turn them down. If you're lucky, you'll be the one carrying the drugs, if not, you'll be the bait, the expendable one they tip the cops to. They'll be busy arresting you as the real mule gets a free pass. In Louisiana it's thirty years for simple possession, thirty ... fucking ... years."

"What'll I do?"

"Don't hang around here." José surveyed the street. He was afraid to be seen with me. Then he pushed his face towards mine. "Go home."

The next day John and I were on a plane to Winnipeg.

Home

Steam wafted from my shoulders
as I walked from the jet to the terminal. The bitter cold burned my
face. I probably shouldn't have worn my jacket on the plane. Every
drop of sweat down the middle of my back froze. Winter in Winnipeg.

Airplanes, beeping machinery, mobile stairs to nowhere, baggage
carts, and people. Hundreds of silhouetted people, all standing on
the airport's balcony, their breath rising like steam from an army of
kettles. Cheers momentarily drowned out by jet engines ripping the
frozen air. John points, a dozen hands wave back. I recognize a few
and wave.

In the terminal the crowd is wall to wall. My parents and brothers
are there. John's parents also. The newspapers are there. We babble
something unintelligible to the reporters. Flashbulbs go off. We pose
with our knapsacks. Our parents hug and kiss. The mayor shakes
our hands. I hug my mother and cry into her perfumed shoulder as
people pound my back.

After the initial euphoria the crowd lingers a while, then disperses.
The smiles melt to nods of recognition. Friends begin to leave and I
get in my parent's car and go home.

John and I never look at each other.

For two years after the trip, John and I didn't speak.
We never mentioned each other, never once tried to get together. The
year I got married, John and I bumped into each other at the Avenue
Restaurant, a hangout from our high school days. For the first time

since New Orleans we sat and shared a meal. I watched him eat his sandwich and a smile came over my face.

"So tell us about the trip," Bev, the owner, said. You didn't disobey Bev. In her little café, she was queen. She once ordered the school's vice principal, who was looking for truants, to leave the restaurant unless he was going to order something. Meanwhile, a dozen students cowered in the kitchen. What Bev wanted Bev got.

Haltingly at first, then with more and more enthusiasm, we regaled her. We ended up with a small crowd hanging on our words. We've never stopped talking about the voyage.

I was John's best man at his wedding. Even though we live a thousand miles apart, we talk regularly. While I was writing these stories, I would email each completed chapter asking for his comments and suggestions.

"Rance, you do have a way with words," he wrote back once.

Some things never change.

Photo Credit: Larry Ranson

John and I at the Winnipeg airport, arriving back home. Note that John's bag is still soaked from the Mississippi.

Photo Credit: Isabel Ranson

Being interviewed by a reporter at the Winnipeg airport. My father, Larry Ranson, is on the left. The Mayor of St. James, Bill Hanks, is standing between me and the reporter. "Mayor Bill" got the city to pay for our flight home.

Note to self: If you are ever going to be interviewed again, practice some sound bites – what came out of our mouths was unintelligible. It sounded like we had spent the last three months on a riverbank.

▲

On the left is my father, Larry Ranson. I am being kissed by my mother, Isabel Ranson. Rick Selby, son of "The Rev" in Chapter One, is looking on. The little boy with the US army helmet is my brother, Mark Ranson. I bought this helmet in New Orleans for one Canadian dollar.

RICK RANSON, the third child in a family of six children, was raised the son of an enthusiastic, story-telling Royal Canadian Air Force Captain, and grew up in military bases across Canada, from Vancouver to Labrador. When he was 16, Ranson hitchhiked from Winnipeg through the US to Toronto, and then from Winnipeg to Mexico, before canoeing from Winnipeg to New Orleans. After a brief stint in Australia (1974-1975), Ranson settled in Winnipeg, MB, where he lives today.

Ranson has worked as a longshoreman, a drill ship's welder, a boilermaker, a farm equipment salesman, an editor for McGraw Hill, a forklift operator, and a business owner. Ranson has contributed to several publications, including *The Cottager*, *Gam on Yachting*, *Western Producer*, and *The Herald*. He is also the author of *Working North: DEW Line to Drill Ship*, which chronicles the eight years Ranson spent working as a welder in the Canadian Arctic.

▲

I, John A. Van Landeghem, on the 25th day of November, 1969 do agree to purchase one half of a red, 16 foot fibre-glass canoe called "Chimo", from Rick Ranson for the price of $50.00

This money is to be paid to Rick on or before the 31st of June, 1970; or on or before a one month time period has expired, on my return to Canada. Depending on which comes first.

SIGNATURE of RECEIVER — Rick Ranson
Rick Ranson

Signature of Payee — John Van Landeghem
John A. Van Landeghem